La Bella Vita

LIFE, LOVE AND FOOD
IN SOUTHERN ITALY

VIDA ADAMOLI

summersdale

LA BELLA VITA

First published in 2002
This edition copyright © Vida Adamoli, 2006

The right of **Vida Adamoli** to be identified as the author of this work has been asserted in accordance with sections 77 and 78 of the Copyright, Designs and Patents Act 1988.

Condition of Sale
This book is sold subject to the condition that it shall not, by way of trade or otherwise, be lent, re-sold, hired out or otherwise circulated in any form of binding or cover other than that in which it is published and without a similar condition including this condition being imposed on the subsequent publisher.

Summersdale Publishers Ltd
46 West Street
Chichester
West Sussex
PO19 1RP
UK

www.summersdale.com

Printed and bound in Great Britain

ISBN 1 84024 489 5

Includes eighteen mouth-watering recipes that will bring the magic of the Mediterranean to your kitchen

ACKNOWLEDGEMENTS

Love and gratitude to Julian, Lucian, Sarah and Cherry for sharing their richly detailed and evocative memories. This book could not have been written without them. Thank you also to my agent, Lisa Eveleigh (who never gave up), and Greg Wales who suggested writing it.

For Enzo
And in memory of Francesca

CONTENTS

CONTENTS

Preface

THE BEGINNING

At eighteen, visibly pregnant, I married my Italian boyfriend at Holborn Registry Office. A year later we said goodbye to CND marches, dolly birds and London's Swinging Sixties and took our baby son to Rome. As befits a romantic Jewish girl from Golders Green my fantasy was a picturesque garret in some ancient cobbled back street of Trastevere. I did not get it. What I got was an apartment within walking distance of Lorenzo's office in the modern Parioli area.

Then, as now, Parioli is known for its bourgeois affluence. Our thirties' block, however, was one of the ugly and run-down exceptions. For a rent of over half our meagre monthly income we had three boxy rooms and a bathroom infested with huge black cockroaches. The living room and bedrooms overlooked the communal garages, while the kitchen looked out on a singularly dank and stinking patch inhabited by diseased chickens and a bald, scabby, evil-looking dog.

This fetid backyard belonged to an old prostitute with dyed ginger hair who lived immediately below us. I had nothing against prostitutes, I thought them exotic in fact, but the first time I knocked on her door to retrieve a dropped Babygro, it was clear she was a woman to avoid. As it turned out, much time and practice was needed before I mastered the precarious art of hanging over a balcony and pegging clothes on to a washing-line. So like it or not, I bothered her often.

Mutual dislike simmered dangerously for several months. Then the bald dog got entangled in a pair of my knickers and we had a near punch-up outside the concierge's cubbyhole. At its climax Lorenzo, my mother, the prostitute's mother and her most assiduous client were involved. There was much fist and handbag waving, and she threatened to gouge out Lorenzo's eyes with the stiletto heel of her scuffed black shoe. The confrontation was loud and dramatic but stopped short of actual blows. At one point the client, a squat Mussolini lookalike, announced he was a high-up police officer and would see us all in jail. He didn't, so I presume it was just a boastful lie. My neighbour, however, was a problem I could cope with. The blistering summers I could not. And the main reason our tempers reached boiling point that day was because so had the weather.

Mid-July temperatures in the city were lethal. The pavements reflected a heat so dizzying I'd find myself clinging to my son's pushchair all the way home from morning trips to the market. As bad, if not worse, were the nights. Drenched sheets twisted around restless limbs and attempts at conjugal intimacy were a complete waste of time. By August I knew better than to venture out after 10 a.m. While my husband found respite at his air conditioned desk, the baby and I barricaded ourselves behind closed shutters. At hourly intervals we plunged into a cold bath, after which I threw myself dripping and naked onto the marble hall floor hoping a draught would come wafting under the front door.

The Romans' response to this climatic peaking is mass exodus. The fortunate go to villas in the mountains or by the sea, the rest to relatives living anywhere vaguely rural. Women and children decamp when the schools close, husbands stoically sweat it out until they can join them at the weekends. Everyone takes their annual holiday in August. Shops and restaurants close, newspaper kiosks shut down and in our area running out of cigarettes meant walking for miles.

Being poor, our summers depended on the hospitality of relatives, either in London or with my mother-in-law in an Abruzzi hill town. Then in spring 1968, with a family now consisting of two sons aged six and two, we joined a friend for a day out. It was driving towards Naples with the car roof down and on the lookout for a new picnic spot that we discovered Torre Saracena (or rather, to protect the village and the people whose stories I tell, this is what I choose to call it).

Our first sight of Torre Saracena came suddenly as we rounded a bend. Directly in front of us, perched on the top of a sheer rocky promontory, was a whitewashed castellation of buildings outlined against a cobalt backdrop of sea and sky. It took us only a few minutes to reach it and even less time to fall in love.

We spent a magical day on the deserted beach. On the way back to the car we stopped at a tiny *alimentari*, dark, cool, smelling of wine and damp straw matting, crouched in the shadow of an ancient, boarded up church. Behind the counter a young woman in a crisp white apron was stuffing green olives with fat slivers of garlic and putting them into a jar. Her name was Benedetta and she would soon become my first Saracenesi friend. I told her I thought Torre Saracena the most wonderful place on earth and asked if she knew of any cheap accommodation for rent. 'I'll take anything,' I declared passionately. 'All I ask for is running water.'

For a moment my eagerness took her aback. Then she said that there might be a place – although not an apartment exactly – in the house opposite her own. She explained that it belonged to a widow who kept it for the use of her sister when she visited once a year from America. As the sister had not been for a long time, however, it was now always empty. I begged to see it immediately. Still bemused by my enthusiasm, Benedetta agreed. She called the small girl playing outside to mind the shop, left the olives, and telling me not to 'expect anything special', led the way.

The place wasn't 'special' and it wasn't an apartment, but to us it was perfect. It consisted of one large room with a toilet and hip bath behind a rickety partition on the balcony. Access to the windowless kitchen below – once a storeroom for wine and oil – was via a door at the bottom of the communal stairs. Best of all, the rent for the three summer months was the equivalent of what my husband spent in the same period on cigarettes.

The boys and I moved in on a perfect June day and stayed until October, arriving back in Rome just in time for the first day of the autumn school term.

We had found paradise: a tiny, unspoilt village caught in a time warp. We were eager to be part of it, to love it, learn from it, enter into its customs and rhythms. What we couldn't know then was that like the settlers who brought the measles virus to the indigenous Americans, we were introducing the virus of the twentieth century. We were part of a small vanguard which heralded an invasion that would change the nature of Torre Saracena forever.

Chapter One

THE FIRST YEAR

The last year Torre Saracena belonged exclusively to the Saracenesi was 1968. It was still poor then but not desperately so. A more stable economy had been established in the fifties when greenhouses were erected on surrounding land to supply the Italians' insatiable demand for year-round tomatoes. Nobody went hungry any more and most households had shop-bought clothes and the odd labour-saving gadget. The extra cash, however, brought only superficial differences. Traditions and the ingrained habits of centuries remained unchanged. People fished, worked the land and charted their lives by weddings, baptisms and funerals. Women and girls carried great baskets of laundry on their heads to wash in the freshwater stream that ran below the promontory into the sea. Old men idled away the hours outside Giovanni's bar in the main Piazza or on the low bridge wall. Old women with inscrutable faces sat like watchful black crows on their doorsteps darning stockings or crocheting. There was television now, of course, and a little open-air cinema overlooking the sea next to the secondary school. But gossip continued to be the village's lifeblood and principal diversion.

Torre Saracena's history reaches back more than two thousand years. Its first inhabitants fled the low-lying plains, building their walled citadel high on the jutting headland where command of miles of sea and beaches provided a safe haven from the savagery of marauding pirates. The village suffered many incursions – the most devastating led by the infamous Barbarossa (Redbeard) in the early sixteenth century – and pirate stories and legends are at the heart of Torre Saracena's cultural history.

Torre Saracena's architectural influence is Greek-Moorish. Houses are whitewashed, windows small and recessed, doors and shutters painted blue or light green. No cars or motorised vehicles of any kind venture past the Piazza. The streets are either steep staircases or narrow winding corridors forming a honeycombed maze leading through low arches and tunnelled walks to the blind, hidden corners where unsuspecting intruders once had boiling oil poured on their heads. The walls are feet-thick and plaster is moulded with no sharp corners. Buildings curve and flow into each other and everything is an essential structural part of the whole. It is a world of its own, a life folded in on itself, a clenched stone fist.

Our apartment was in Via S. Leone, the main thoroughfare that ran past the old church, through the east archway and down to the developing new town below. Five feet at its widest, it is paved with large round stones worn slippery smooth and shiny by generations of feet. The buildings are four or five storeys high, with an occasional jutting protuberance where a bathroom was added later.

By the time we arrived some of the choicer properties had already been snapped up by discerning *forestieri* (foreigners – a term used to describe anyone not from the village or its immediate vicinity). These precursors of the tourist boom were still just a novelty presence, however. And to the Saracenesi, for whom efficient plumbing, Formica and a modern kitchen represented the domestic dream, anyone mad enough to spend good money restoring rotting beams and cracked terracotta floors solicited amused – even contemptuous – disbelief.

One of the first conversions had been done by an elderly Milanese woman who lived obliquely opposite us. She had bought the property over ten years previously and her tiered garden running down to the Belvedere was a riotous profusion of flowering cacti, geraniums and purple bougainvillea. I knew her as a paragon of virtue and on one occasion got the sharp edge of her tongue for returning from the beach with only a T-shirt over my bikini. But according to Benedetta she had not always been so. In her past she had been a vaudeville actress and her liaison with a high-ranking Fascist (shot by partisans after the war) had been given wide coverage in the popular scandal magazines. I heard versions of the same story from Signora Teresa who ran the Emporio and also from Brunetto il Piccolo.

We called him Brunetto il Piccolo because he was just over five feet tall. He was 29 then, fair, with the long solemn face of a much taller man and large, very pale blue eyes. A fisherman from the age of nine, Brunetto had recently been hired as an odd-job man and gardener by the rich American expatriate who now owned the old mill at the bottom of Via S. Leone. 'Much better,' he told me. 'More money, less work.'

We became friends after an incident when he stepped in to stop Marcello, my eldest, from being beaten up by the much older postman's son. After that Brunetto started taking Marcello to the open-air cinema once or twice a week (for some reason he got in without paying) and every so often he brought me knobbly thick-skinned lemons and wild garlic from the mill garden. In return I invited him into my kitchen for English tea and we would talk until I became too tired and had to go to bed. Our conversations always started with a detailed recital of the most recent film's plot and ended with him lamenting his romantic woes.

The boys and I quickly established our daily routine, which varied only slightly when Lorenzo joined us at the weekends. We woke at seven and breakfasted at half past, after which I prepared our sandwiches. Due to financial restrictions, these invariably consisted of a single slice of mortadella, or scraping of cheap processed cheese, topped with masses of lettuce and wedged between doorsteps of rough, crusty bread. By eight thirty, loaded with towels, books, buckets and spades, we were already treading the stony path down to the beach.

That first year we camped outside Tullio's. His establishment was a long wooden shack where we bought drinks and used the makeshift hosepipe shower. It was no real rival to Leone's 300 yards further along, but it was cheaper. Tullio, a big bear of a man with an unpredictable temper, was rumoured to have been in a criminal asylum for murder. On his release he had squatted a section of the beach and the shack, which he built single-handed, was a place of surprising charm and beauty. A single, largish room, it had a fireplace at one end and a bar at the other. It was painted pale green and sky-blue, and decorated with driftwood and other odds and ends thrown up by the sea. The whole family slept there but where they kept the beds was a mystery. The only visible furniture consisted of a couple of trestle tables for the clients who came to eat the simple fish dishes his wife prepared in the primitive kitchen tacked on the back. She was thin, downtrodden, and often complained to me about how hard her life was. Her main grievance was that Tullio still had not started on the extra room he had been promising her for years.

For the villagers the beach was a place of work, not recreation. It was where boats and nets were mended, where the catch was brought in and where linen was washed and spread on rocks to dry. Some people also believed they could cure ailments there. Signora Piera, for example, came down to bury her fat varicosed legs in hot sand for half an hour or so each day and there was an old man who did something similar for his rheumatism. For the most part, however, the beach was still left to the enjoyment of stray dogs, passing Nordic hitch-hikers and a few holidaymaking families from Rome and Naples. That year, even in July and August, it was a majestic sweep of uncluttered splendour.

Of the handful of umbrellas at Tullio's, the grandest had a gold-tasselled edge and belonged to a 20-stone Neapolitan woman and her daughter-in-law, Rhona. Rhona, who came from the Midlands, had an eight-month-old daughter and was as delighted as I was at the chance to talk English. Sprawled on the sand, waves lapping our toes, we began our acquaintance discussing children, in-laws, money and the merits and faults of our respective husbands. Within a few days, however, Rhona introduced the topic of sex and our conversations became much more interesting. We also had a friendly rivalry going as to who could get the better tan. As I seemed to be getting darker quicker, she forewent her sun creams and used my much cheaper concoction of cooking oil and weak tea (we thought it so brilliant we even talked about marketing it).

At around one thirty the boys and I gathered up our things and left. With the heat at its fiercest the steep climb was too much for Luca and I always ended up carrying him: an exercise which left me bathed in sweat and with every muscle quivering. We arrived to a village shuttered and deserted for the long siesta. Only the occasional cough or sound of dishes being washed up disturbed the silence. There was a special magic about walking home at that slumbering hour. The intense glare of the sun bleached everything of colour, and shadows cast by houses divided the streets into razor-sharp zones of dazzling white and deepest black. It was like wandering through an abandoned stage set, almost too sculptural and picturesque to be true.

Back home we collapsed onto the straw mattresses and slept too. At about four the village awoke again. Children shrieked, toilet cisterns gushed, women held shrill conversations across balconies, radios and televisions blared, pots and pans began clashing again in preparation for supper and there was the constant *slip-slap* of slippered feet on polished stone. Another familiar sound was the grating bump of Saverio's home-made wood and tin wheelbarrow. Saverio was Benedetta's uncle and earned a few lire running a delivery service for anything too heavy to carry. Fifteen years before, he told me, he used to have a donkey to do the work.

Benedetta, slight and pretty with perfect teeth and thick, dark, glossy hair, lived with her parents, grandparents and various siblings in the house directly opposite. On the day we arrived she called in to say hello and give the boys a sugared doughnut each. Her bedroom window was on the same level as our balcony – almost close enough for us to shake hands – and we often chatted across the gulf.

On her grandmother's ninetieth birthday she invited me in for a glass of sweet wine and an almond cake. In the main room where the family was gathered heavy, dark wood furniture gleamed in the shuttered half-light. Through an open door I could see a large terrace looking out over the sea. Grandma, swollen legs encased in black woollen stockings and resting on two feather cushions, sat in the only armchair. A smell of polish and mothballs mingled with that of cinnamon and nutmeg and the rich aroma of percolating coffee.

'Your house is beautiful,' I told Benedetta.

'It's too old-fashioned,' she replied shyly, shaking her head. 'I would like to make everything new.'

Later she took me up to her bedroom and proudly showed me her bottom drawer. I was very impressed. Her towels, sheets, pillowcases and table napkins were all of the finest, whitest linen. She had embroidered the entwined initials of her fiancé and herself in pink and gold on the corner of each item. She had been courting her *fidanzato* for eight years but had only recently become officially engaged. 'I'll be married this time next year,' she confided, adding darkly, 'if Gino doesn't put a jinx on things, that is.'

'Why should he do that?' I asked.

'Because Gino brings misfortune, that's why,' Benedetta replied. 'He can't help it; it's how he is.'

Gino, the hunchback, lived in one tiny room where Via S. Leone curved down towards the east archway. It had no windows and through his open front door you could see the shrine he had made to the Virgin in a niche by his narrow bed. When he wasn't working for Renzo the cobbler, he swept and reswept his bit of street with a long twig broom. His obsession was litter, which he was forever accusing people of dropping. Many times I was angrily confronted with a piece of screwed up paper on his outstretched palm. As he only spoke dialect – which I never managed to master – I couldn't tell whether I was being accused or simply shown the sins of others.

Gino's unfortunate reputation was not only due to his deformity. It went back to his father being struck by lightning just hours after he was born. Benedetta said there were earlier signs too, like his mother's hair falling out while she carried him in the womb. She also said that when he had stayed with an aunt as a small child, a mysterious fire had all but burned the place down.

It was the belief that he brought bad luck to lovers that was most widespread, though. It was said, for example, that a girl who crossed his path after trying on her wedding dress would never reach the altar. Or if a girl accidentally brushed against him in the street, she had to perform a special ritual to exorcise the romantic hex he had passed on. Another one said that if he engaged a couple in conversation on the first night of the full moon, their marriage bed would be forever cursed.

His friendship with *la finta suora* (the false nun) – a harmless mad old woman who dressed as a nun – didn't help much either. Like Gino she was also considered an *iettatore* (bringer of misfortune), though mostly by the very young children who had great fun screaming and scattering when they saw her approach. I personally thought they made a touching couple. They often sat together on his doorstep and she helped him shell mounds of broad beans and sweet young peas when they were in season.

The Piazza – not to be confused with the New Piazza built twenty years earlier outside the original entrance to the village – is the nerve centre of Saracena life. It was where Signora Rosalba and Signora Annamaria set out their vegetable stalls and where the touring market originating in Naples still arrives early every Saturday morning. Giovanni's bar is on the corner, flanking broad stairs that fork on the left to the Belvedere and on the right to the main route down to the beach. Nestled in the fork was Signora Teresa's Emporio, a small room crammed with sewing equipment, rubber flip-flops, cheap plastic beach toys, jars of liquorice, sherbets, bubblegum and tiny sweets that the children bought by the handful for a few lire. In the Piazza there was also a butcher's, greengrocer's and a shop selling wine and gas cylinders. The following year the tobacconist and Salvatore's cake shop also moved their business there. The Piazza was an exclusively male domain, as was the bar. It was a place for cards, gossip and heated political debates. Women and girls kept to their doorsteps or balconies and, up until a decade previously, old women still only used it to cross from one place to another.

I followed the village example. I only went to the bar at weekends, escorted by Lorenzo, except for the one occasion when Brunetto il Piccolo invited me to join him for a coffee. The bar belonged to Giovanni but most of the work was done by his middle-aged daughters, Pina and Claretta. The only customers he was prepared to serve personally were his coterie of old friends: weather-beaten, gnarled patriarchs with large bellies and callused hands who occupied the chairs lined up along the outside wall. Giovanni was a small, wiry, bad-tempered and uncompromising old man, invariably dressed in short-sleeved shirts, knitted sleeveless pullovers and baggy trousers hitched high under his ribs. The first and almost only time I saw his toothless laugh was the occasion I rushed into the bar as it was closing, gashed my forehead on the half-closed shutters and nearly knocked myself out.

Thanks to my friendship with Brunetto il Piccolo I knew all about the conflict raging between Giovanni and Peppino that year. Peppino was a lecherous and decaying Neapolitan playboy whose connection with the village went back to before the war. Several years earlier he had taken over what was left of the old gatehouse on the south side of the Piazza and was now planning to turn it into a bar. According to Brunetto there was more to the question than simple business rivalry. Firstly, until the Neapolitan came along and offered to rent it, Giovanni had used the gatehouse (which was owned by a third cousin) as free storage space. Secondly, there was the incident when Giovanni kicked Peppino's dog. Except it wasn't really about that, it was about Giovanni's wife.

Giovanni's wife was rumoured to be the fattest woman in the entire region. Nobody outside her family had seen her for nearly forty years and Giovanni's explanation was that she was too wide to get through the front door. But this, apparently, was not the full story. In her youth she had been a beauty famous for her green eyes and luxuriant mane of tawny hair. Giovanni had won her in the face of fierce competition and after the marriage spent the rest of his life guarding his prize. She began putting on weight while carrying Pina and with every pound his obsessive jealousy grew. She was only allowed out if chaperoned by an elderly female relative – preferably his mother – and then only to the shops or church.

Complications developed after Claretta's birth and Giovanni's wife had to go to the hospital in Matia. Brunetto's grandfather, who was one of Giovanni's closest friends, helped Giovanni and the doctor carry her to the horse-drawn cart waiting in the Piazza. Despite the fact it was a scorching August day he insisted on smuggling her out in a blanket; the risk of suffocation preferable to any male eyes getting a glimpse of her abundant flesh. She stayed in hospital for almost six weeks and after her return neither went out nor was seen at her door or windows ever again.

The incident with Peppino's dog happened after it slipped its leash while Peppino was walking it to the barber's. Peppino was always receiving complaints about the dog, considered by the Saracenesi, who do not keep pets, as a useless pest. To avoid more trouble he immediately gave chase, collaring it in the blind corner off Via della Madonna where Giovanni had his house. Giovanni arrived while Peppino was on the narrow walkway running from the top of a short flight of stairs to his front door. At the sight of Peppino Giovanni went into a mad frenzy and kicked the dog so hard he cracked two of its ribs. I was appalled at such cruelty to an animal. Brunetto, however, pointed out that in the circumstances it was lucky that was all that had happened. 'After all,' he said, 'the old man thought Peppino was sniffing around after his wife. If he'd had a knife he'd have killed both of them.'

At the end of September, just before we left to return to Rome, a wooden plaque was erected on the gatehouse wall with 'Bar Peppino' burnt into it in ornate letters. A flurry of activity followed. The interior was cleared and painted, a marble-topped bar installed and rustic trestle tables appeared. Its progress was followed with great curiosity and Peppino told everybody he was opening for business the following spring. He planned that the handful of 'foreigners' – who, like himself, were not catered for – would form the nucleus of his clientele. We would all be invited to the inauguration, he told me grandly, to partake of *spumante* and *tartine* on the house. I thought this sounded very nice. Our landlady had agreed to rent us our place all year round, so I knew we would be there.

But when spring arrived Peppino's bar did not open. Giovanni had discovered that the gatehouse was owned jointly with another cousin who lived in Marseille and who nobody bothered to inform about anything. Giovanni immediately wrote to tell him about the proposed plans and, more importantly, point out that for many years he had been deprived of his rightful share of the rent Peppino paid. As a result, old grievances were resurrected and a full-blown family row ensued.

Peppino used all his Neapolitan wiles – and a few cash sweeteners – but to no avail. It took two years before things were sorted out and the reconciled cousins gave him the go-ahead. By then the number of foreigners had increased tenfold. It was not really surprising, therefore, that when he finally opened his doors the promised free bash was conveniently forgotten.

Panzanella

I did get to enjoy Peppino's hospitality on one occasion, however. I was hanging around the piazza hoping to waylay a plumber when Peppino beckoned me over. He wanted to show me how the Gatehouse refurbishment was progressing. It was early days and the place looked like a building site, with chalky-smelling distemper still wet on the walls. It was gone noon and a makeshift table was set up for lunch. '*Prego, prego,*' Peppino put an arm round my waist and urged me forward. '*Mangia un boccone con noi.*' When I hesitated the paint-splattered young man washing his hands spoke up. '*É roba buona, signora,*' he assured me, '*Lo ha preparato la mamma.*' So we all sat down, wine was poured, and I found myself tucking into my first-ever *panzanella*, or Tuscan bread salad. It was a culinary revelation.

Feeds 4

1.5 kg (3 lb 5 oz) stale casareccio bread (alternatively sourdough/ciabatta)
800 g (1 lb 12 oz) firm, juicy, plum tomatoes, diced small
1 large sweet onion, sliced fine
Big bunch of fresh basil, roughly torn not chopped
Extra virgin olive oil
Salt and pepper

Break the bone-dry bread into chunks and soak in water. After 15 minutes or so squeeze all water out and place the moist, crumbly bread in a large bowl. Mix in the chopped tomatoes and sliced onion with olive oil and season to taste. I personally add the basil at the last moment to keep it from wilting.

Chapter Two

THE BIG BANG

It was in 1969 that it finally happened. From the late forties on, an insidious trickle of infiltrators (like ourselves) had slipped through the cracks, but this was the year Torre Saracena's charmed isolation was violated forever. Overnight Giovanni's bar became an open-air *salotto*, the Piazza a stage for impromptu life dramas and, before the summer was out, a pitched battle was fought in the narrow streets between left-wing activists and local fascists. For the village it was the tumultuous dawning of a new age, the assault of the microcosm by the macrocosm. The heraldic reverberations summoned film-makers, actors, intellectuals, eccentrics and the rebellious young. Old men like Giovanni said Torre Saracena had fended off Turkish pirates only to be invaded by something worse. Brunetto il Piccolo saw it as a great opportunity for getting ahead. We thought it incredibly exciting and called it the Big Bang.

My first intimation of this historic disruption was in early May when I came for the weekend to prepare for our summer stay. A leak from the bathroom upstairs had saturated one wall of our room, rotting two pillows and a pair of my sandals, and everything smelt damp, musty and generally unwelcoming. Sand had blown in drifts through the crack under the door and a spectacular cobweb was looped around the flex of the naked light bulb hanging from the centre of the ceiling. For the next couple of hours I swept, dusted, washed the floor with a mixture of water and bleach and lugged our unwieldy straw mattresses (Luca's still reeking of pee) onto the balcony to air. Several radios were tuned in to the Vaticano station and a stereo effect 'Ave Maria' resounded all down the street. At eleven thirty – the magic hour for mozzarella connoisseurs – the prayers stopped and the priest started talking about missionaries in Africa. I downed tools and hurried to Benedetta's shop.

Eleven thirty, twelve at the latest, was when the daily batches of fresh mozzarella were delivered from local buffalo farms. That day they were punctual as usual, arriving in two battered old plastic buckets; warm, succulent, and sloshing in milky liquid. It was the treat I had been anticipating since the moment of boarding the early morning train. Without waiting for them to be transferred into glass bowls and put on the counter, I selected a perfect white oval the size of my fist and devoured it greedily there and then. Benedetta, who had watched me do this many times, never failed to be amused by my eagerness and the way I let juice squelch messily all down my chin.

Her mother was sitting on a stool in the doorway salting anchovies and pressing them into a deep stone jar.

She was a short, thickset woman, pretty like Benedetta, with clear bright eyes and grey-streaked black hair coiled into a bun. When I complimented her on how well she looked, she confided that her doctor wanted her to go to Rome for a kidney-stone operation but she had told him it was too far away and she did not believe in operations anyway. Her late father, she said, had suffered the same thing and had cured himself with herbal infusions. On his sixty-fifth birthday he passed a nugget the size of a large apricot and she could show it to me to prove it. I asked what the infusion was composed of. 'Wild garlic, I think,' she said vaguely. 'Maybe carob and bay leaves and probably a bit of chilli pepper, too.' Then, changing the subject, she wagged a finger and warned, 'If you're planning to go to the beach watch out for the foreign gypsies camping near Leone's. A more disreputable, ragged lot you've never seen.'

It was a subject they had obviously been discussing because Benedetta sighed and pulled a face. 'I've told you, they're not gypsies, mama. They're friends of Billy's from New York.'

'What difference does it make where they come from?' rebutted her mother in an aggrieved tone. 'They're here now! And anyway, I don't believe Billy has friends like that.'

Several other women had come into the shop and echoed her view. 'Billy's a gentleman,' one of them stated emphatically. 'And I'm in a position to know. He's been helping my Enzina with her Latin homework for years.'

Billy was Belgian and for some reason enjoyed the rare privilege of being accepted by the village as one of its own. I had first noticed him sitting alone at a table outside Giovanni's. He looked incongruously urbane and elegant in a white linen suit with Quincy, his big Labrador crossbreed, sprawled at his feet. I was also intrigued by the fact that, apart from his clique of old cronies, he was the only customer I had ever seen Giovanni chatting to with any animation.

Brunetto il Piccolo told me that Billy had come to the village several years earlier with a local boy he had met in Florence. There was talk he had been ill, a mental breakdown it was said, which was why the boy's mother took him in and looked after him like a son. He lived with the family for over a year, then rented the two small rooms he now occupied at the top of the house next door. Despite a tacit acceptance that Billy's relationship with his friend was homosexual, it had not affected people's attitudes. And when the boy later got married, Billy contributed financially to the wedding and stood as godfather to his first child. There was some envy about his money, however. Brunetto speculated that he was supported by a rich family because he had never been seen to do a day's work. Billy's family *was* rich, as it happened, but I found out later that he was also a writer and had published several books. Furthermore, the ragged bunch of foreigners were indeed his friends. Or, rather, Stella was.

Stella was from Venice where Billy had met her in 1957. He was 17 and had just arrived from Brussels. She was 29 and girlfriend-cum-personal assistant to a titled art collector. Despite the age difference they hit it off immediately and when he decided to move to Florence she dumped the art collector and left with him. Then in 1960, on what should have been a two-week holiday in New York, she fell in with a crowd of avant-garde young actors, one of whom she later had a child with, and decided to stay. She kept in touch with Billy, however, and on her first trip home she made a point of coming to Torre Saracena and looking him up.

On leaving the shop I went straight to the beach to have a look at the 'foreign gypsies', but couldn't find them. I looked for them again on a second visit later in May, this time bringing sheets, towels and a giant pasta pot. In the end I didn't get to see them until the day we all arrived for the summer. By then they were no longer camping as Brunetto il Piccolo had arranged for the Big House in the Piazza (once the Town Hall and long shuttered) to be reopened and given to them for a peppercorn rent.

We arrived on 10 June at about five in the afternoon. Staggering into the Piazza with our baggage, the first thing we noticed was a group of four men, three women and a girl of about five lounging outside Giovanni's drinking Cokes. In their caftans, embroidered waistcoats, flowing skirts, bandannas and abundant jewellery, they were a flamboyant sight. Passing women gave them dark, sidelong glances and muttered unheeded warnings to the giggling and gawping children. The small, scrawny, cross-eyed road sweeper – whom I had often seen beating his young sons with his broom when they got on the wrong side of his violent temper – had planted himself in the centre of the Piazza and was regarding them with a savage stare. As soon as he spotted us he scuttled over bellowing raucously, 'Look at that lot over there! The American Circus has come to town!'

Although suspicion and hostility prevailed, Billy's friends were also regarded as a novel source of entertainment. They spent a lot of time at Giovanni's drinking, playing guitars and generally having a good time. I observed them with as much curiosity as anybody else, but we only became acquainted after my 16-year-old sister arrived with three friends and I had a row with Pina over a broken glass.

Although I did not actually witness the incident, I was given a detailed account of it. During a high-spirited evening spent at the bar my sister Louise accidentally jolted the table, knocking her glass to the ground and breaking it. What upset her was not the fact that Pina charged for it (although she knew it had been provided free by the Peroni brewery). It was the public humiliation of Pina's screaming diatribe.

The following morning I left the boys in Louise's care and steamed up to the Piazza to confront Pina. There were no preambles and we locked horns immediately. The set-to started across the bar counter, but the vehemence of our passion demanded a larger arena and we soon found ourselves outside. It was a typically Latin confrontation. For half an hour or so we shouted and gesticulated in each other's faces, neither listening to a word the other was saying. Not that it would have made much difference if we had. Pina chose to express herself in broad dialect and my uncertain Italian metamorphosed into a weird, fantastical language of its own. The essential meaning behind it all, however – the clash of cultures for which we were demanding respect – was crystal clear to both of us.

Rage, like love, tears through social barriers. It leaves polite restraint in tatters and creates an intimacy all its own. At a certain point we found that the identities of 'Saracenesa' and 'forestiera' we had given each other were no longer valid. Like it or not we were forced to acknowledge each other as individuals. In fact, it was during this raw and violent exchange that the foundations for mutual esteem and our subsequent friendship were laid.

During the heat of the row I lost all sense of time and place (like the scene in *West Side Story* when Tony and Maria meet at the dance and everything around them dissolves into soft focus). When I came to afterwards, I discovered we had attracted a large audience, including Giovanni's old codgers who had vacated their seats in order to follow the altercation better. I also noticed that several of Billy's hippy friends had arrived and were regarding me with grinning admiration. 'That was brilliant. Street theatre at its authentic best,' one of them enthused when Pina went back inside. 'Yeah,' agreed another. 'But what the fuck was it all about?'

So I sat down and told them. Throughout the story the little girl with them frowned at me fiercely. When I finished she took her thumb out of her mouth and informed me that her name was Claudia and she liked 'pasghetti'. She went on to introduce the others as Ringo, Del, Elvira and Jasper – 'my papa'. Her mother, she said, was called Stella and she was down on the beach looking for sea urchins with Arthur and Jan. When I told her that I had two little boys, one of whom was her age, she leapt up and insisted we went to see them at once.

'Show her how you roll your belly first,' commanded Jasper.

'OK,' she said, obediently pulling up her flowered shift and, to much laughter and applause, making her little brown tummy undulate sinuously. I tried to laugh with them, but I had never liked seeing children being made to perform and found her party trick disturbing.

By now my anger had subsided and I was aware of the need to re-establish civil communication. So before taking Claudia to meet Marcello and Luca, I went back inside the bar to face Pina again. It was a quiet moment and she was sitting on a stool behind the bar crocheting what looked like a place mat. I complimented her on the fine, intricate work.

'Women here learn to crochet at their mother's knee,' she said. 'I suppose it's different where you come from.' I agreed it was. 'Well, never mind. If you want I'll teach you sometime.'

She presented me with a conciliatory cappuccino with a liberal sprinkling of powdered chocolate on top. Then she told me that Salvatore, a young man from a nearby hill town married to one of her cousins, would soon be opening a *pasticceria* on the opposite corner of the Piazza. Apparently he had learned his trade from an uncle who worked for a famous pastry chef in Catania. As she talked I nodded and smiled. It was as though no cross word had ever passed between us.

By now Billy's friends were not the only new faces around and each week brought more. There was the burly Florentine sculptor, Nato Palmieri, who looked like Richard Harris and who once confided that in his mid-teens he had supported himself by selling sex. His male clients, he said, all came from Florence's aristocracy. His wife Jane, a sophisticated Canadian journalist, was half his size but looked so much like him that at first I took them for brother and sister. Then there was their friend, Tommaso Rossi, a professor of philosophy at Bologna University who persuaded Rick, a painter from Glasgow on a scholarship to the British School in Rome, to paint him as a satyr. Rick agreed – for a fee – but when the picture was completed Tommaso refused to pay and they quarrelled about it for the rest of the summer. Rinaldo, a charming Neapolitan scoundrel, came first on his own and then returned with his pretty wife, Florrie, and their new baby. A well-known Greek actress who fled her country after the military coup turned up in mid-July with a much younger lover, followed a few days later by a contingent of political exiles from Argentina. But the real excitement was the arrival of Danny the Red, famous leader of the May '68 student uprising in Paris, and his entourage of fellow revolutionaries. He was just 22, charismatic and to me hugely attractive.

The Piazza had always been the village focal point, but now it was even more so. Giovanni, resentful of the extra work and dismissive of the money it brought in, was vexed to find his bar crowded all morning and from eight onwards every night. The number of tables he was obliged to cram under the tree more than tripled and Pina and her sister, Claretta, persuaded him to take on Nino, an engaging 12-year-old, to help them serve. The newcomers gathered there to read radical publications, debate politics, eye up possible sexual partners and generally scrutinise everyone else. Leone's, not Tullio's, was the beach place to go, and night parties with dope and nude bathing became a frequent event. The air fizzled with excitement. Everybody was experiencing the same thing – the discovery of Torre Saracena and each other – at the same time. It was like being part of a unique, intoxicating, grand scale love-in.

For the villagers, of course, it was different. They looked on with suspicion and alarm. For the older ones the new *forestieri* had the mark of the Devil stamped on their foreheads – especially when rumours of the nude bathing got around.

'You have to understand,' Brunetto il Piccolo explained, 'the women here are modest even with their husbands. My mother, for instance, wears black stockings even in the height of summer. Now she sees girls in miniskirts sitting at the bar smoking and drinking with men. To her it's Sodom and Gomorrah.'

The historic street battle took place on a Saturday night at the end of August. Not being brave, I spent most of it watching from our balcony with Louise and her friends. Lorenzo, however, was right in the thick of it and for a couple of weeks wore his battle scars like trophies. It was triggered by a photo of Danny drinking coffee at Giovanni's that appeared in *Il Secolo*, the Fascist daily newspaper. The contemptuous caption read: 'So-called French Revolutionary, Danny Cohen-Bendit, Chooses Torre Saracena for Bourgeois Holiday.' Fascists throughout the region were roused to a clamouring fury. They let it be known that they considered his presence in their territory an insult and a challenge, which meant trouble was expected. When it came, however, its magnitude took everyone by surprise. About fifty Blackshirts arrived in the Piazza shortly before midnight armed with a menacing array of knives, chains and cudgels. This punitive raid, coordinated by Saracenesi Fascists, was mounted not only to 'give the Red shit a lesson he wouldn't forget'; it was also seen as an opportunity to get coverage in both the local and national press.

For several hours the narrow streets echoed with hoarse cries and pounding feet. Ambushes were sprung, missiles thrown, and people trapped in blind alleys were kicked and beaten. Lorenzo clashed with Elio, a hulking six-footer, who broke a chair over his head, giving him a gash that needed several stitches. The skirmish lasted until 2 a.m., when the police finally arrived and everyone scattered. No arrests were made but Danny and his entourage were given three days to leave town.

In small communities people learn to coexist with fellow citizens – not to mention family members – of diametrically opposing political views. And they certainly have more in common with a political opponent they've grown up with than those sharing the same views but from somewhere else. On this occasion, however, loyalty to fellow villagers and embryonic outrage at the foreign invasion was temporarily suspended. The war that night was exclusively between the Left and Right. The comrades of Torre Saracena fought alongside their outsider counterparts, and even blood relatives found themselves exchanging blows.

Tension was still running high the following day. Every phase of the battle was analysed and those with personal testimonies were repeatedly called upon to give them. At every corner groups of villagers argued fiercely about the incident from their respective political standpoints.

Lorenzo and I ran into Elio on our way back from the doctor's surgery. He was already sorry for the injury he had inflicted.

'I only got involved because my brother, Tonino, made me,' he explained with a rueful grin. 'You must have seen from the way he struts around he thinks he's Il Duce himself.'

Lorenzo was not a man to bear grudges and they shook hands, declaring no hard feelings on either side.

From then on Elio took to walking around with a copy of *L'Unita*, the official Communist newspaper, tucked ostentatiously under his arm. But I found it harder to forgive. In fact, another couple of years passed before I relented and we became friends.

In September the exodus started. People returned to their city lives and of the New York hippies only Jasper, Stella, Claudia and Ringo remained. They loved the village, loved the Big House, and had decided to stay and make it their home. Jasper and Ringo had signed up for an underground film scheduled to be shot in a concrete bunker-like villa owned by the German director's girlfriend a few miles down the coast. Claudia, by then moderately conversant in both Italian and dialect, was enrolled for the autumn term at the local elementary school. For her part Stella said that after nine years grafting in the Big Apple all she wanted was to sit on her bum all day. Pina's opinion of it all was the same as most of the locals. 'What can they do here?' she asked. 'Why should they want to stay? They'll never fit in.'

A lazy, end-of-season atmosphere prevailed now. Like everyone else, I rarely went down to the sea in the mornings any more, preferring to sit around chatting and reading newspapers at the bar. Anyway, the beach, like the Piazza and Giovanni's, had become another *salotto*, a place for toing and froing between umbrellas and congregating on Leone's veranda. Leone enjoyed having us around and was delighted when Jasper painted the wooden columns supporting the veranda roof to look like Indian totem poles. He joined in our card games and occasionally provided feasts of stale bread moistened with water and topped with slices of the tomatoes his father grew on their land at the back. There were six brothers and two sisters and the youngest brother, Gino, then about eight, had made himself a drum kit out of petrol cans. Although he kept it in a shed half a mile away, his frantic drumming could be heard all over the beach. Rick, the Glaswegian painter, thought he was brilliant and was inspired by his example to make a bamboo flute. Thereafter they often played together and Gino wept bitterly when he left.

For the children the beach, like the village itself, was a magical playground. Nato showed them how to make sand volcanoes by lighting a fire in an underground cavity and sending billowing columns of smoke out through a hole in the top. Jasper found a long plank of wood and fixed up a makeshift diving board on the little outcrop of rocks in front of Leone's. This got the children's vote as the most exciting feature of that summer and they spent hours hurling themselves off it. They staged battles too, excavating dugouts from which they bombarded each other with balls of wet sand. Marcello and Claudia had become close friends. She also enjoyed hanging around with me. One of her favourite things was to help me wash clothes in the cavernous marble sink opposite the toilet on our balcony. On one occasion I gave her a pile of Marcello's socks and T-shirts to tackle. Halfway through some vigorous scrubbing she announced that she had decided to marry him when they grew up. 'Why?' I asked.

'Because he's so filthy I'll have to do piles of disgusting washing all day long,' was her rapturous reply.

Around that time Brunetto, by now a fledgling property agent, took us to see a flat for sale. It was owned by a Signora Petroni from Rome who proudly maintained it was the village's first-ever conversion. Situated on the opposite side of the Piazza from Giovanni's, it consisted of two rooms, one on top of the other, and a tiny roof terrace with a view across rooftops that tumbled in steep tiers to the sea. The downstairs room had no direct window but a marvellous terracotta floor. The upstairs room incorporated a kitchen corner and had a balcony overlooking the Piazza just big enough for two pots of leggy geraniums. We loved everything about it, including the price: £2,500. My mother had recently divorced and was still undecided as to what to do with her share of the sale of the family house. I immediately began inundating her with letters and phone calls. On the strength of my enthusiastic description – and the assurance she could earn money renting it out – she decided to buy it unseen.

The transaction was fraught with difficulties, the main one being that Signora Petroni was constantly changing her mind about whether she wanted to part with the place after all. In fact, shortly after the contracts were finally signed, I found her gazing up at the flat with tears streaming down her face. When I recounted this to Pina, she pulled a face. Signora Petroni was the most tight-fisted person she had ever met, she said, and was only crying because she knew that if she'd waited another year the flat would have sold for twice as much. 'I remember the winter she spent here with her mother,' Pina told me. 'The old woman was almost eighty but to save on gas her daughter would only let her cook a hot meal twice a week.'

That winter involved much coming and going with tedious, time-consuming practicalities like registering the sale at the new Town Hall and transferring electricity and water rates into my mother's name. On one of these trips our new neighbour, Signora Lucia, told me that as owners we would now have to share the cost of whitewashing the communal stairs. Every villager, she explained, took responsibility for whitewashing their stairs and bits of wall. It was an ancient tradition and one of the reasons Torre Saracena was so beautiful. She was a friendly, talkative woman. We often chatted from our adjacent front doors and in the end it was she, not Pina, who taught me to crochet. One afternoon, however, while I was waiting for the bank to open, Pina instructed me in the lost art of darning a woollen sock. Although it is a skill I never use, I am proud to own it and will always be grateful to her for passing it on.

Puntarelle in salsa di alici

For me Benedetta's mother's salted anchovies were the tops. Sometimes I mashed them in a pan with oil, garlic and red chilli pepper and served them with al dente spaghetti. And they made my *puntarelle* (Catalonian chicory tips) *in Salsa di Alici* sublime.

Feeds 4

*800 g (1 lb 12 oz) puntarelle (alternatively frisee or
other curly-leaf lettuce)*
8 salted anchovy fillets
2 cloves garlic
2 tbsp red/white wine vinegar
4–6 tbsp extra virgin olive oil
Salt and pepper

Cut the *puntarelle* lengthwise into thin strips. Put the strips into a bowl of cold water and leave until they turn into pretty curls. Chop the garlic and anchovies into small pieces and mash with the vinegar (a mortar and pestle is good for this). Now add the olive oil a splash at a time, working the ingredients into a smooth paste. Rinse the *puntarelle*, drain them and spin dry. Place *puntarelle* and anchovy dressing in a large salad bowl, mix thoroughly and serve.

Chapter Three

JASPER'S YEAR

Torre Saracena in winter is another place. Its beauty is shabbier, less resplendent, more sombre and elemental. Without the bleaching intensity of the fierce summer sun, it is a greyer shade of white, and ancient blocks of unadorned stone knuckle bonily through a worn, flaking skin of streaked whitewash. And when the great storms come, when the looming hills press in blackly, when the sky heaves and boils and cracks and shudders, when the rain crashes against closed shutters and the narrow streets dissolve into fast-flowing rivers, when the electricity fails and plunges everything into darkness, then the village battens down its hatches, becomes again a clenched fist, a sharp, stony bastion against raging, primeval chaos.

We arrived for our first off-season weekend of the year in just such a storm. The bus scheduled to meet the late afternoon train at Matia was almost an hour late (due, we were told later, to three of the four tyres needing an emergency change). Across the flooded station forecourt was a small bar that served the men who worked for the local Agricultural Co-operative. It also sold eggs laid by lively chickens that scrabbled around in a garden at the back. Grabbing children and bags we made a frantic dash for it. It was empty except for a tiny old lady huddled by a paraffin stove and a young man with a smiling moon face dreamily rolling a pair of ivory dice on the scrubbed counter. Lorenzo and I ordered two large black coffees. The boys – soaked to the skin and shivering – insisted on lemon ice lollies. I smiled at the old lady and pushed the boys closer to the stove. She stared back vacantly for a moment with milky, cataractous eyes, then suddenly shrieked, 'You silly fool, you shouldn't have come! The good Lord's creating all this fuss to punish you for your wickedness!'

'Be quiet, grandma!' the young man barked. Then he shrugged apologetically and tapped a finger to his temple. 'Take no notice of her, she's out of it. But who knows if the bus will come at all in weather like this? Still, I can drive you if you want. I do a bit of taxiing on the side.' It was a tempting offer but the sum he wanted, though reasonable, was more than we could afford. Reluctantly we declined and settled down to wait.

The bus did turn up eventually: a blue, rusting relic from the fifties that looked as though it might fall apart at any moment. There was a further delay as the stationmaster was called out to move his car so the bus could effect its wide, grinding U-turn. And then we were on our way, clanking, rattling and shuddering along the narrow, pot-holed road that led through flat fields to Saracena Mare and on up to the old town above. On either side, through streaming windows and thunderous gloom, we could see the sheets of silvery polyurethane that covered the tomato-filled greenhouses lifting and billowing like ghostly sails in the buffeting wind.

'Look!' exclaimed Marcello to Luca, half malicious, half in awe. 'Pirate ships! You'd better watch out.'

The ticket collector was the husband of Signora Rosalba (the lady from whom I bought my vegetables). A robust, handsome man in his mid-fifties, he was wearing a long oilskin jacket and a black knitted cap pulled down to his eyebrows. He looked very fierce.

'You're the one who'd better watch out,' he said to Marcello. 'And forget about pirates. I'll slit your throat with my cut-throat knife if I catch you charging up and down my steps like you did in the summer!'

The only other passenger was Saverio, Benedetta's uncle, on his way back from Matia. He showed us the huge, red-handled chisel he had bought and asked if we were going to stay at our place in Via S. Leone or my mother's new flat. When we told him the latter, he said, 'You'll need a fire on an evening like this. I can bring you a barrel of wood if you like. It'll only cost you a thousand lire.'

I was ready to hum and ha but Lorenzo immediately agreed. I was grateful that he did because when we got in we found that the roof had leaked in at least six places. There was a pool of water inches deep at the bottom of the stairs and the chair and mattress in the upstairs room were sodden. (I didn't know it then, but my mother's leaking roof and our efforts to get it repaired were to be the leitmotif of all our Torre Saracena years.) To make matters worse, Saverio's wheelbarrow turned out to be too wide for the steep flight of steps leading to our door, so we all put plastic bags over our heads and carried the timber up in armfuls.

We built a fire in the cavernous grate with wood from chopped up wine casks. It caught immediately, filling the room with warmth and a spicy, fecund aroma that intoxicated us. While Lorenzo and the boys unpacked I cooked a pasta supper on the two-ring gas cooker tucked away on a tiled ledge behind an arch. It was rich with garlic, chillies and thick green olive oil and we ate with bowls on laps and our feet propped up on the raised hearth. The electricity had failed again and the town was plunged in darkness. I had forgotten to bring candles and the only light was that of the fire. Mellowed with wine and food, we gazed entranced into its crackling, incandescent heart. Around us guttering tongues of shadow licked a restless path over the rough plastered walls and beamed ceiling. Outside the storm continued its rampage. Inside it was cosy bliss.

The next morning it was all over. The sky was a clean, eggshell blue and children floated matchbox boats in puddles that dazzled with reflected sunlight. With the departure of the summer people, village life had quickly resumed its normal routine. The beach was once again the domain of stray dogs, fishermen and the women who filed down the stony path to wash clothes in the icy freshwater stream. We found Giovanni looking almost cheerful. The hated outside tables were stacked away in the back room of the bar where he now spent every afternoon chain-smoking Nazionali and playing cards with his cronies. He was no longer harassed by foreigners requesting bizarre beverages and his clientele had reverted to being more or less what it had always been.

But the Big Bang had happened. The village had been rocked by the carnival clamour of its great Coming Out Ball and that was not easily forgotten. As Brunetto il Piccolo said gleefully when he came to pay us a visit, 'The Wind of Change is blowing our way at last and I'm going to take advantage of it.' He went on to explain that he was officially setting himself up as a renter and seller of flats. Furthermore, for a small fee, he would also take care of people's property while they were away. He left us with a spare set of keys to my mother's flat and the conviction that his new career had just got off to a kick-start.

Claudia came to see us that morning too. She had started at the local elementary school and was so enamoured of her new regulation black smock and white nylon neck bow that she never took them off. She was fluent in Saraceno dialect by now and particularly relished the swearwords. When Marcello refused to give her half of the gum he was chewing, she came out with a stream of curses, including *pouzzitt lu seng* (which roughly translated means 'may your blood turn dry in your veins'). Luca's reaction to this verbal assault on his adored older brother was to sink his teeth into her arm. Marcello, however, was mightily impressed. After a token scuffle they retreated into a corner and struck a bargain. She would get the gum she so ardently desired – but only after teaching him every curse and insult in her repertoire.

Her father, Jasper, had not made such impressive linguistic progress (and never would). We found him sitting with the old men outside Giovanni's giving an animated account of a fishing trip he had taken with Elio, the man who hit Lorenzo over the head during the famous riot. His means of communication involved a lot of gesticulating and the adding of o's and a's to the ends of English words. Every now and then he would inject a '*Tu capisc'*?' and a resounding '*Porca la miseria*!' While he was describing the huge jellyfish he had landed, the ex-mayor seized every pause to reply with a story of his own about a motorbike his son had bought. Despite the fact neither knew what the other was going on about, both clearly found the conversation perfectly satisfying.

We were returning from Benedetta's with provisions for the weekend and had stopped at the bar for a glass of the local white wine.

'Hey!' Jasper called, spotting us. 'Nice to see you guys. But you don't want to bother with that stuff', he said, gesturing towards the Big House. 'Come into my castle and have a real drink with the King!'

Lorenzo accepted with alacrity, leaving me to struggle home alone with the shopping and join them later. Halfway across the Piazza I met Signora Lucia with a basket piled high with carrots and potatoes on her head. She stopped to stare at Jasper strolling over towards the 'castle' with Lorenzo. Despite the bright sun it was not a warm day and Jasper was showing a large expanse of bare midriff between his green velvet waistcoat and flowing cotton trousers.

'Just look at that *americano*,' she said contemptuously. 'Now you tell me, Signora – what sort of man is it that goes around with his belly hanging out?'

The occupation of the Big House by Jasper and company was as shocking for the Saracenesi as Martians taking over Buckingham Palace would be to the British. At one point it had been the Town Hall and was a rambling, three-storey warren of rooms. The grandest of these was on the first floor, with a balcony overlooking the Piazza and a faded fresco of birds and flowers garlanding the vaulted ceiling. It was furnished with a couple of yellow foam pouffes and a low table made from two planks of wood supported by several large tins that had once contained tomatoes and were now filled with sand. The 'real drink' was on this table: three bottles of Southern Comfort donated, Jasper said, by Chuck and Hank of the nearby US naval base.

By the time I eventually arrived, one bottle was sinking fast and a furious game of cards was underway. Apart from Jasper and Lorenzo, the other players were Billy, Ringo and another pal from the naval base, an Italo-American called Roberto Buonarotti. I didn't want to drink and there was nowhere for me to sit so I joined Stella who was preparing vegetable soup in the dark cave of a kitchen. She was wearing a forties' floral print dress from a second-hand market stall and her bush of grey-streaked frizzy hair whizzed around her head like a demonic halo. I thought she looked wild and wonderful and I told her so.

'Thanks,' she replied dryly. 'It makes a change to get a compliment. Everywhere I go here I'm followed by evil little brats yelling "Witch! Witch! Witch!"'

She showed me around the rest of the house. Most of the rooms were empty; a couple had the odd piece of nondescript furniture. The one she and Jasper slept in, however, had been transformed into a royal bower. The walls were hung with swathes of brilliantly coloured silks and embroidered Indian hangings (theirs), and in the centre was the most magnificent bed I'd ever seen (the house's). Made of heavy brass, it had naked nymphs curled around

51

the four bedposts and a winged cherub rising with outstretched arms from the centre of the headpiece. I just couldn't resist. I flung myself down on it and for a few magic moments pretended to be a princess.

On the top floor were two interconnecting attic rooms leading out onto a large roof terrace. It commanded an aerial view of ochre roofs and narrow passageways snaking out from the Piazza, down to Saracena Mare on one side and the beach on the other. We were standing in the corner where two sides of the stone balustrade met. It was like being on the prow of a great ship breasting a path through a sweeping arc of glittering sea.

'Look,' said Stella. I followed her pointing finger to the long curve of beach far below. Near the etched spread of fishing nets, three tiny figures ran happy, zigzagging circles on the rain-darkened sand.

'Our crazy kids,' I said, laughing. 'Shall we join them?'

The next day was Sunday. The modern church in the New Piazza was broadcasting a cracked recording of St Peter's bells (the priest thought the church's own were insufficiently grand). Most of the village, including many of the Communists, attended mass. The women wore their best outfits with neat plaited buns covered by headscarves, the men wore sober suits, some of which dated back twenty years or more, the children were well scrubbed and immaculate. We watched their procession from the covered terrace of Bar Sole, the 'winter bar' on the bridge (so-called because its sheltered balcony allowed one to sit outside most of the year). Luca, who had recently started attending a nursery school run by nuns, demanded to be taken to the service too. I explained that we weren't going because we were not Catholic. He was most put out and began to grizzle. When Lorenzo told him to shut up, he retorted piously, '*Suora* Benedetta says Jesus gets angry when nasty daddies make his little creatures suffer!'

In the afternoon it clouded over again. We lit another fire, less fragrant this time as all the wood from the wine cask had been used up. Marcello and Claudia did their homework (Claudia chewing her pencil in anguish over three times six), while Luca drew a blue and red stick figure with a long streamer flowing out of its neck. 'It's Superman,' he informed us gravely. 'The biggest, strongest superhero in the whole world.'

Later Stella came by with a packet of biscuits and I made steaming mugs of hot chocolate for everyone. At five we had to leave. It had started raining again and the air was filled with the gushing and gurgling of water coursing down myriad gutters, gullies, steps and drains. It sounded as though the village had sprung one gigantic leak.

We only managed a couple more weekends that winter. Rome held us captive with school, office, and the sundry worries of everyday life. While I struggled to be an adequate Italian housewife – which had much to do with not overcooking the pasta – Lorenzo did his best to provide for us and keep the wolves at bay. Our survival, however, was principally due to the tradition of endless credit extended by all *alimentari* (grocers) and, particularly, our own Signor Spigoni.

We were back by 1 May, however. Labour Day is an Italian national holiday and by the artful construction of 'bridges' – the annexing of days either side of a holiday to a Sunday – we had four whole days at our disposal. By then the weather was glorious and we arrived hungry for the electric rush that the first, exhilarating sight of virgin beach and shimmering expanse of sea always gave us. We also found ourselves swept up in the excitement as the village prepared for the celebrations taking place the next day.

Most of the activity was centred on the Piazza. One team of men was constructing a 15-foot-high wall of wire netting a few yards from the bottom of my mother's steps. Another, with garbled directions from Jasper, struggled to erect a 20-foot pole decorated like a Native American totem pole. We immediately recognised his signature on this flamboyant piece of artistry – a fact that he eagerly confirmed when we hauled him off to the bar for a beer.

'Yeah, it happened like this,' he said, sweating, breathless and proud. 'I got hold of Cristoforo [nephew of the ex-mayor and one of the people responsible for the organisation]. "Man," I said. "Man, you can't just stick up any old pole and leave it at that! That pole," I said, "is the centre of everything. It's the maypole, after all. The goddamn cherry on the whole goddamn cake!" The guy just stared at me, he didn't have a clue. "Relax, Cristoforo old buddy," I said. "Don't worry. Just leave it to me."'

'That's right,' agreed Ringo. 'Three of us carried the thing back to the house and it's been parked half in, half out of the living room for the past month. The first design was pure Sioux but we kept on changing it and it's a mixture of influences now. Right, Stella?'

Stella had been listening to all this with her customary closed and impenetrable expression. 'Indeed,' she said, with deadpan sarcasm. 'It's been a long business, but I think we all agree Jasper's come out a real star.'

As it turned out, Jasper was to prove himself a 'real star' the next day. From eleven in the morning the Piazza started filling up and by midday the whole village was there. Children crowded steps, walls and perched in the branches of the tree outside Giovanni's. Those of us with windows overlooking the Piazza shared the privileged view with friends or family.

The festivities kicked off with speeches from assorted local dignitaries, then went straight into the Wire Wall event. The blindfolded contestants were allowed two attempts to strike out at the random array of earthenware crockery hung on the wire. The flailing sticks mostly missed the targets, but when they did succeed in hitting one it was usually found to be full of water that soaked the victor (or victim) to the skin. A lucky few found a plump salami, a round of goats' cheese, a sugared doughnut or a packet of washing powder among the shattered shards. Some also contained tiny paper-wrapped sweets that scattered like hailstones and were fought over by a stampeding rush of whooping children. But the big prize, the one everybody lusted after, was tied to the top of Jasper's now thickly greased pole: a whole leg of *prosciulto crudo*. At least thirty of the village's young men were stripped to the waist ready to contend for it. And the new challenger among them, with a pocket-sized American flag sewn on the back of his jeans, was Jasper.

One by one they attempted the climb. Anyone who managed to reach the halfway mark before backsliding was allowed another attempt. By three o'clock there was only Elio (the reigning champion) and Jasper left. Because they consistently passed the mark, they were eligible to assault the pole again and again. By this time the crowd had reached fever pitch excitement. Although most of the village was rooting for Elio, Jasper had a loud contingent of supporters of his own.

From the very start of his victory ascent everyone knew instinctively that Jasper was going to make it. He was slower, more dogged and purposeful. And when he started to slide three-quarters of the way up he didn't struggle, but locked feet, knees, arms and head and hung on with grim determination. For several long minutes he remained clinging like a desperate limpet 15 feet above the ground. Then inch by agonising inch, urged on by the chants of his supporters, he dragged himself up to the summit, stretched out a trembling hand and touched the ham. The crowd exploded with a deafening roar. A forest of hands were waiting to grab him as he slithered to the ground. He was hoisted onto strong shoulders and borne away for a triumphant tour of the town. Children showered him with paper streamers, teenage girls gave him shy, giggling smiles, men stopped to pat him on the back and say, '*Bravo americano!*' Elio, philosophical about his defeat, kissed Jasper on both cheeks and declared magnanimously, '*Amico mio*, now you are one of us.'

As for the ham, it turned out to be riddled with maggots. But Jasper was undismayed. He got Benedetta to slice it up anyway and invited everyone he met to the Big House for a celebration party. It was a rowdy affair during which Jasper insisted on performing his own potted version of Shakespeare's *Macbeth*. On finishing, he poured a bottle of wine over his head, and solemnly declared himself Jasper I, Torre Saracena's new Thespian King.

Fave fresche al guanciale

By the time of the May Day festivities *fave* (broad beans) were in season. Each morning Signora Rosalba and Signora Annamaria piled their stalls high with the green, nobbly pods. When they were young and fresh we ate them raw with slivers of pecorino cheese. When they got too tough for that I stewed them with *guanciale* (a fatty unsmoked bacon made from the pig's jowl).

Feeds 4

800 g (1 lb 12 oz) shelled broad beans (I don't take the outer skin off after shelling)
150 g (5 oz) guanciale, diced (alternatively thick-cut smoked streaky bacon)
3–5 tbsp extra virgin olive oil
2 spring onions, finely chopped
Cup of vegetable broth
Salt and pepper
Crusty bread to serve

Fry the spring onions in the olive oil together with the diced *guanciale*. Add the broad beans, season with salt and pepper, and cook over a low heat with the lid on. Every now and then add a few spoonfuls of vegetable broth. When tender serve with good crusty bread.

Chapter Four

SIGNORA LUCIA'S DAUGHTER STARTS COURTING

Next to village gossip, Signora Lucia's favourite topic of conversation was illnesses: her own and everyone else's. In this she was not alone, for all the village women (and men too, for that matter) seemed to find the subject similarly fascinating. Her particular interest was the complications and suffering of women giving birth. Although she knew a hundred gory stories, it was with a special relish that she recounted her own. She referred to Maria Immaculata, her daughter, as a 'gift from God' because she was born when Signora Lucia was 45 and her husband, Gaetano, 53. By that time they had been married for 25 years and were long resigned to being childless. In fact, when her periods stopped she simply presumed she had started the menopause. 'I knew at my age the birth wouldn't be easy,' she would say with a tremulous flutter of her small, plump hands. 'But such pain and agony, *signora mia*, no mortal being is prepared for!'

Her labour, she claimed, took 36 hours and when the crucial time finally came the doctor was off administering to someone else. Fortunately for everyone, however, one of her sisters-in-law was on hand to take charge. Tiny, no taller than four foot ten, Signora Lena was formidable in everything but stature. Not only had she delivered herself single-handedly of two babies (one of which dropped while she was harvesting olives halfway up a stony hillside), but she had been called on many times to act as emergency midwife to others.

On the night of Maria Immaculata's advent she was assisted by relays of female neighbours and relatives. While some squeezed up and down the narrow stairs with jugs of boiling water, others hovered near the bed supplicating the Madonna to hurry things along. When the baby finally emerged the problem became clear – the poor thing's head was 'as big as a prize pumpkin'. This ordeal left Signora Lucia not only exhausted to the point of delirium, but literally 'torn to shreds'. There was muttering among the women watching as to whether she would make it but her sister-in-law did not turn a hair. She merely sterilised a darning needle over a candle flame and stitched her up with coarse black thread.

The blood, Signora Lucia would say, savouring the dramatic recollection, spilled out of her like a river bursting its banks. Signora Lena packed her vagina with ice cubes right up to the womb but it still took three days for the haemorrhaging to stop. Her main regret, still fresh and poignant after all the years, was for her mattress. 'I'd put a rubber undersheet on it, of course,' she would sigh, 'but it was still ruined. Old Giacomo made it of the finest quality wool for my trousseau. It took my mother two years of scrimping and saving to pay off the debt. Throwing it away broke my heart.'

Signora Lucia first told me this story in the summer of 1971 after witnessing a visiting friend of mine mistake indigestion for premature labour on our communal steps. Maria Immaculata, who was stirring a tomato sauce in the cubbyhole kitchen by their front door, listened with such rapt attention I concluded (wrongly) that she had never heard the details of her birth before. She was now a pretty, obedient 17-year-old whose head, though nicely rounded, was no longer particularly outsized. An avid reader of gossip magazines, she amazed me with her passionate interest in the English royal family. Her special favourite was Prince Charles and her main leisure pursuit seemed to be updating a scrapbook of his photos. When I asked what it was exactly she liked about him, she said he was 'really good-looking' and 'every girl's dream'.

Signora Lucia agreed with her daughter's judgement. She was something of a royalist herself and had nurtured a similar admiration for Italy's last king, Vittorio Emanuele III. 'He was only a little man but he cut a dashing figure in his uniform,' she said. 'I went off him, though, when he turned tail and fled in 1943. Well, prince or pauper, no woman likes a coward, does she?'

I put Maria Immaculata's bizarre crush on Prince Charles down to the restricted life she led. Shackled to elderly parents, she was forever busy with one domestic chore or another with no time off for normal teenage fun. I was often sorry for her – especially when I felt her big, wistful eyes on me as I tripped down the stairs on my way to the bar or beach. Consequently, the last thing I expected was to return one late afternoon and find her sitting on her narrow doorstep thigh-to-thigh with a good-looking young man. But this surprise was nothing to the wonderment I felt when she proudly introduced him as her fiancé, Nando. Given that Maria Immaculata never went out – and certainly nobody came to visit – where on earth had he sprung from? And when and where had she been doing her courting?

That I should be so perplexed reflected my ignorance of the fundamentals of village life. For as Benedetta told me the next day, Maria Immaculata and Nando had in fact been wooing since they were thirteen and fifteen respectively. She knew this because her sister, Paolina, had been in Maria Immaculata's class at school. 'They might have put a man on the moon, but things don't change much here,' Benedetta said. 'It's not like Rome or Naples. Our ways are still the ancient ways.'

The presence of her mother sitting on a stool in the doorway prohibited her from elaborating. Later, however, she explained in more detail. In Torre Saracena passion and desire inhabited a secret place. It was communicated by veiled glances and smiles, fugitive exchanges after Sunday mass. Outsiders like myself were blind to this subtle language of inference and nuance. We were unaware of the turbulence constantly raging beneath the tranquil surface of village life. In this context the love story of Maria Immaculata and Nando was commonplace: gazing, yearning, and the long, achingly chaste years of wait. It was when she left school and relieved her mother of the burden of taking the washing to the stream that the relationship took a physical leap. Which was why the families had decided to make it official – one person too many had reported seeing them sidle off to kiss and cuddle behind the rocks.

The traditional courting route for engaged couples was the steep road that crested the hills coasting the sea. The view was spectacular and it was far enough from the village to allow a small measure of romantic privacy. Young men and women strolled it at least once a week, with a chaperone straggling a discreet ten yards or so behind. Delighted though they were that Maria Immaculata and Nando now qualified to join their ranks, it presented her parents with a problem – who was to accompany them? Since suffering a minor stroke a few years earlier, Signor Gaetano had adopted a rigid policy of minimum exertion. His total energy expenditure was the daily walk to his chair outside Giovanni's (about twenty paces) and a rather longer haul to the church in the New Piazza on Sundays (about two hundred). Signora Lucia, who claimed countless ailments, was short and fat and the knotted clusters of varicose veins on her legs were agony. Furthermore, it was the height of summer and even in the late afternoon a walk up that road was a daunting business.

Signora Lucia, however, loved her daughter very much. She also approved of her prospective son-in-law and was therefore prepared to sacrifice herself. For the first two outings, wearing new shoes and a smart navy and white patterned two-piece, she trudged heroically up the hillside behind them. On the third occasion she had an unfortunate encounter with a billy goat and ended up in a ditch. According to Maria Immaculata – who had been both upset and embarrassed by the incident – the animal butted Signora Lucia because she kicked it to make it get out of her way. Signora Lucia hotly denied this, however, maintaining the animal was malicious and the attack entirely unprovoked. Be that as it may, the outcome was that Signora Lucia was too bruised and shaken to accompany them again.

Finding a replacement chaperone was not easy. Signora Lucia was 62, Gaetano 70, and all their various brothers, sisters and in-laws were ranged in age between 55 and 80. This meant that they were all either suffering some incapacitating ailment or simply disinclined. In the end it was the cousin of the husband of one of Signora Lena's granddaughters who agreed to step in until a solution was found.

Nando, the *fidanzato*, was a fisherman like his father and had six brothers and sisters. The only one I knew was Mario who worked in the trattoria situated opposite the chemist's shop (a dark, cavernous place with dusty shelves and an ancient wooden counter etched with the deep cuts and scratches of a century or more) situated at the entrance to the village. At that time it was the only eating place in the old village and my sister, Louise, and her friends spent a sizeable whack of their holiday money there. They almost always had the same thing: chicken roasted with garlic and rosemary and served with a mound of crispy fried potatoes. Because they were so predictable, Mario took to greeting them with a loud bellow of 'Chicken and chips – *giusto*?' the moment they came through the door. This amused them hugely and 'Cheeken and Cheeps' – as Mario pronounced it – became their nickname for him.

Mario flirted with all the foreign girls but Louise was the one he went after most persistently. She was 17 but with her round face, dimples, unruly curls and general air of virginal innocence, most people (Mario included) assumed she was two or three years younger. Despite this, he still saw her as 'fair game', one of the fantasy foreign females Italian males of that era associated with guiltless, available sex. This meant that while his brother's courtship of Maria Immaculata followed all the rules of respectful reserve, Mario's definitely did not.

His main objective was to persuade Louise to go dancing with him at the Blue Demon, a sleazy bar in the large port town further down the coast. Failing that, he wanted to take her for a walk in the hills; not the courting route, but the one that wound inland past the slaughterhouse to the freshwater spring, and without a chaperone, of course. To this end he harassed her relentlessly when he succeeded in cornering her on her own. He made personal comments about her appearance, saying that her bottom was the shape of an apple or that she must make an effort not to slouch when she walked. What annoyed her most, however, was his teasing insistence that she let him brush her 'naughty little curly hairs'. Apart from anything else, she complained tearfully, his use of the plural and his wheedling tone made the suggestion sound positively pornographic.

All in all it was turning out to be a summer of sexual tensions. For Tammy, the plump nine-year-old daughter of the Tuscan sculptor, Nato Palmieri, and his Canadian wife, Jane, the problem was the premature sprouting of a pair of breasts. Small though they were, the presence of these pubescent buds filled her with shame, distress and a burning anger. Instead of playing with friends, she swathed herself in an enormous Swiss flag and sat, glowering, scrawling rude words in the sand. The rage she radiated was cosmic and all-encompassing. When it found focus, which happened fifteen times a day on average, it was generally directed at her mother. Nato advocated drowning or selling her to the gypsies. Jane just felt awful. 'The kid holds me personally responsible for what's happening to her body,' she said miserably. 'I guess one day she'll realise it's not my fault she's growing up... won't she?'

Parenting Tammy in her present frame of mind was a draining and thankless task. On one occasion she told me she hated everything about her mother except her sandwiches. Even Tammy had to acknowledge merit there. For Jane's succulent American-style triple-deckers were the envy of all the children on the beach. These lavish concoctions (kept moist by damp linen napkins) featured inspired combinations of chicken, tuna, egg, sweetcorn, mushrooms, lettuce, tomatoes and much more. On various occasions I was obliged to give Marcello and Luca a kick up the bum for scavenging around her umbrella in search of leftovers. Their martyred response was that the nastiness of my dry mortadella doorsteps had driven them to it.

Tammy's suffering was exacerbated by Claudia's persistent attempts to peer down or, worse still, touch her hated front. In fact, the one time she was seen to release her grip on the Swiss flag was when she turned on Claudia and beat her up. This interest in Tammy's breasts, however, was just part of Claudia's new fascination with sex. With innocent audacity she took to speculating about who was in love with whom, spying on courting couples, and asking outrageous questions like 'Do you stick your tongue in Lorenzo's mouth when you kiss?' This precocious interest had been precipitated by a flamboyant cult star of New York underground films who was staying at the Big House. Amongst other things the star was adamantly against all forms of censorship, including moderating her conversation when an eight-year-old was around. And to further enlighten the little girl she not only answered her questions but drew explicit action pictures as well.

As Claudia considered Marcello her best friend (she still intended to marry him and spend a blissful life washing his filthy clothes), it was natural that he should be the first person with whom she gleefully shared her new knowledge. Marcello had been told the facts of life around the time of Luca's birth. The information had interested him briefly before being thoroughly forgotten. Consequently Claudia's revelations, coming as they did out of the blue, both shocked and disturbed him. Lorenzo and I had left for a week's holiday in Austria, so we weren't there to give him the reassurance he subsequently needed. Fortunately my sister was. She recounted the conversation – which caught her completely off guard – as going like this:

'Louise? How are babies made?'

'Well, what have you heard?' Her instinct was to be cautious. Marcello's explanation was brief and biological. 'That's right,' Louise agreed. 'That's exactly how it happens.' Relieved it had all been so simple she then changed the subject, asking if he wanted biscuits spread with Nutella for tea.

But for once Marcello was not distracted by talk of food. Watching his frowning face work through a complex of emotions, it struck Louise that his worst fears had just been confirmed. Suddenly he narrowed an accusative glare at her and demanded, 'Is that what you're going to do, then?'

'I suppose I'll have to if I want to have a baby,' Louise replied gently.

At this he exploded with passionate dismay. 'Well, don't come and ask me to do it with you!' he cried. 'It's disgusting and unhygienic and I wouldn't do it if you paid me twenty thousand lire!' As Marcello was notoriously greedy, and twenty thousand lire was a mythically enormous sum for him, this more than anything revealed how deeply upsetting he found it all.

Marcello was not the only one upset, however. On my return from Austria it seemed that every other person I encountered was distressed about something. Benedetta, for example, was tearful because her prospective father-in-law had contracted hepatitis and her wedding, finally fixed for the first week of September, would now have to be postponed. Maria Immaculata was in a sulk because the stand-in chaperone had opted out and Signora Lucia refused to let them go walking on their own. Tammy, distraught because she had started menstruating, had been whisked off for an emergency appointment with her paediatrician in Rome. And Louise was angry and exasperated that Mario would not leave her alone.

I empathised totally with Louise's predicament. My first year in Torre Saracena had been one long battle to get local males to treat me as my status as married woman and mother warranted. Back then it seemed that 99.9 per cent of Italian men classified women as madonnas, whores or foreign females (who, although not whores, were thought to behave like them). Italian women, my mother-in-law included, endorsed this last view. In fact, we had a rare row about it the summer Marcello and I stayed with her in the small Abruzzi hill town where she was born. My life there was utterly miserable. No matter how primly I dressed, I could not go anywhere without being propositioned or followed. In the end it was decided I could only go out if I was accompanied by my mother-in-law, her sister, or her sister's elderly maid, Irma.

My mother-in-law, who loved me like the daughter she never had, was outraged at what I had to put up with. Nevertheless she justified her fellow townsmen's behaviour by declaring that 'wantonly shameless foreign women' who, following the advent of mass tourism in the fifties now came in their hordes, had corrupted the Italian male. Before that, she declared, Italian men were noble of heart and intention, treating all members of the gentle sex impeccably. Her sister and Irma agreed, of course, and the conversation degenerated into a slanging match. Outnumbered and outraged, I burst into noisy tears and locked myself in the bathroom. It took much coaxing on their part before I agreed to come out.

Because I understood what she was up against I knew that even a bright city girl like Louise could not deal with the Mario situation on her own. Strictly speaking it should have been Lorenzo who confronted her impudent tormentor, but as he was now back at work the job fell to me.

I turned up at Mario's trattoria at around six in the evening. He was spreading the sheets of white paper that served as tablecloths over an assortment of scrubbed wooden tables. He looked up and smiled, then noticed the ferocious glower on my face. Wasting no time, I launched into a passionate and unrestrained condemnation of his behaviour. How dare he, I thundered, offend the honour and dignity of my young sister by publicly subjecting her to his unwanted attentions! How dare he disregard the integrity of our family by behaving so outrageously! Did he seriously think Lorenzo was the sort of man who would see his sister-in-law insulted and take no action? Would he, Mario, stand by and do nothing if his own sister was pursued in such a way?

My performance was modelled on Anna Magnani and it was very effective. Mario listened without interruption, his expression growing progressively more chastened and pained. At the end of it he made a fulsome apology and, hand on heart, swore never to importune Louise again. He was as good as his word. From that day on he never again so much as glanced in her direction. Louise, greatly relieved, settled down to enjoy the rest of her stay.

By then it was the beginning of September. The sun had lost its razor edge and people were mellower too. Tammy and Claudia spent hours obsessively dressing and undressing the Barbie doll Tammy's grandmother had sent her. In honour of their new best-friend status, Claudia had also started wrapping herself in a flag – a tatty American one of Jasper's. She had little time for Marcello now, who soon stopped worrying about the facts of life and threw himself into exciting gang warfare with the Saracenesi boys instead. And on Saturday, 25 September Benedetta was married.

The ceremony took place at the New Church at ten in the morning. When it was over the bride and groom led the procession of family and close friends back across the bridge into the Piazza. On their arrival the red-faced and sweating brass band clashed cymbals, rolled drums and launched into a lively tarantella. Benedetta, radiant in ivory silk and a frothy net veil, showed no sign of the stress her father-in-law's illness and the postponement of the wedding had caused her. The atmosphere was one of *festa*. The Piazza was crawling with children, including Claudia, Tammy, Marcello and Luca. People watched from windows and women carrying baskets of washing or shopping on their heads paused to heave a romantic sigh. Shopkeepers came to their doorways and even Giovanni's sour old face was softened by a smile. A photographer took official photographs with a tripod camera while the cult film star snapped away unofficially from the Big House balcony. And then the moment the children had been impatiently awaiting finally arrived. The bride and groom produced large paper bags from which to shower the crowd with the traditional sugared almonds Italians call *confetti*.

For such toothsome prizes the fight was predictably fierce. Marcello bloodied his nose, Tammy got a kick in the shins and another small boy was catapulted into Saverio's parked wheelbarrow. But Claudia proved herself a bruiser of the first order. Agile as a monkey, she shoved and elbowed with ruthless determination and within minutes her mouth and pockets were crammed. Hard won though these trophies were, many of the children were prepared to forgo the eating in order to throw them at the big bass drum. The first hail of pink and white missiles was ignored, as were the second and the third. But after a while, when more than one musician had been pinged on the head or nose and, in one instance, eye, the band broke up in disarray.

Shrieking with delight the children ducked and dived as the six men struck out in clumsy rage. One of the cornet players made a lunge at Luca. He was a huge man with a belly as big as the ex-mayor's and Luca sensibly streaked off as fast as his legs could carry him. The old women in the wedding party were also angry, hurling threats and warnings at the brats scattering around their feet. Fortunately the unruliness did not seem to be spoiling Benedetta's day. She was so amused, in fact, that she kept burying her flushed and giggling face in her new husband's shoulder.

I was watching from the balcony of my mother's flat. Signora Lucia and Maria Immaculata were standing immediately below at the top of the stairs.

'There you are,' I heard Signora Lucia say. 'Benedetta's waited eleven years for this day and it's done her no harm. Look how happy she is.' Maria Immaculata, normally so docile, responded vehemently that if she had to wait eleven years she would kill herself.

At that moment her father joined them. 'Women were born to be married,' he declared. 'Therefore it's in their interest to do so as soon as possible. But it's the complete opposite for men!'

And before either of them could respond he shuffled off to Giovanni's bar, chuckling loudly.

Ricotta condita

Benedetta and her new husband honeymooned in Marseille, guests of an immigrant uncle who ran a pizza parlour. On their return I paid a visit to the marital home, an apartment directly below her mother-in-law's. After admiring Benedetta's proudly displayed wedding presents, we sat in her spic and span kitchen sipping marsala and eating this delicious sweet out of pretty cut-glass bowls.

Ricotta cheese
Rum
Very finely ground fresh coffee
Sugar
Crisp little almond biscuits

Put all the ingredients on the table and let each person mash their ricotta in a small bowl with a fork, adding a splash of rum, ground coffee and sugar to taste. Eat with the biscuits.

Chapter Five

TRATTORIA STELLA

Jasper and company's raggle-taggle occupation of the Big House was a continual affront to Saracenesi sensibility. Four storeys high with an imposing balcony and arched portico over the doorway, its flaking grandeur dominated one whole side of the Piazza. The fact it had been empty for over a decade and was in a bad state of repair did not detract from its status as an edifice of historical importance. It had served as the Town Hall from 1945 until the council decamped to their present bunker-like premises in the New Piazza in the early fifties. Before that, and more significantly perhaps, it had been the residence of generations of Torre Saracena's number one family: the Messoris.

The Messoris were the nearest thing Torre Saracena had to aristocracy. Lots of people claimed to be related to them, including the man who kept the draper's shop on the bridge. In fact, the Messoris were one of his two preferred topics of conversation – the other being his acrimonious feud with the owner of the winter bar next door. I received a lecture on them every time I stopped by to rummage through the box of odd buttons he kept on the counter, an irresistible collection dating back fifty years and more. On one occasion he unlocked a drawer and showed me his most treasured memento: a pair of gold cuff links in a silk-lined wooden box.

'From the dressing room of Fausto Messori, a true and noble gentleman,' he said devoutly, going on to describe the family as 'a seam of gold running through two thousand years of worthlessness.'

Not everybody took the same view. Signora Lucia claimed their fortune was a result of voracious greed and the exploitation of villagers kept shackled to penurious serfdom. She recounted the story of a ruthless Messori who forced a newly widowed mother to repay a small debt with the only thing she had – her breast milk. And the cobbler told Lorenzo that the family was as poor as mud until a certain Giacomo Messori gave his two pubescent daughters as concubines to a Neapolitan archbishop in the early eighteenth century. After that, he claimed, money came in by the sackful.

Be that as it may, the Messoris had once owned most of Torre Saracena and the land around it. They were certainly the only villagers rich enough to have their sons not only educated, but educated out of town. Brunetto il Piccolo said his grandfather remembered Alfredo, Bartolomeo and Cristoforo in brown wool suits with high collars being trundled off to their exclusive college in the back of a smelly old donkey cart. That was in 1908. Fifteen years or so later Fausto Messori closed the Big House and, following in the footsteps of his brothers before him, moved his family to Rome. According to Brunetto, the Messori clan were now all doctors or lawyers who lived affluent city lives. They had sold off most of their holdings and rarely, if ever, came home.

Giovanni, like the draper, held the Messoris in high esteem. Not only did he think the *carabinieri* should be called to throw Jasper's lot out, he also stated publicly that he would rather see the Big House crumble to dust than let any outsider live there permanently. Most people took a less radical view. For them a respected professional such as a lawyer, surgeon or bank manager would have been perfectly acceptable, welcome even. It was the amoral tawdriness of the new tenants that most offended the village's communal dignity. That and the much resented fact that it was weirdos, not normal, well-heeled tourists, who were ushering in Torre Saracena's new dawn.

But there was a pro-foreigner element as well. As far as shopkeepers were concerned, customers were customers and goodwill was shown by the odd packet of cornflakes appearing on more adventurous shelves. Saverio's wheelbarrow was now in constant demand and Brunetto il Piccolo was doing brisk and lucrative business letting holiday properties. Many of the young village males were also eager to be part of the new excitement. Elio was one of these. As he said, 'To see life I thought I'd have to emigrate. Now I don't have to bother. Life's coming to me instead!'

Since the May Festival Elio had become an ardent Jasper fan, believing that all that was wild and wonderful in the Big World was embodied in the person of Jasper himself. He looked on with dazzled eyes as Jasper preened, strutted and tossed his lion's mane of sun-streaked blond hair. And he wasn't the only one, for Jasper added to his entourage of admirers daily. Jasper found this deeply gratifying. It was also a relief to have success so easily. New York had been too large, too competitive, too full of people more talented than himself. Torre Saracena, on the other hand, was just the right size; a space he could fill. As he said to Denise (a school friend of Louise's who had a secret crush on him) as they strolled across the bridge to the 'winter' bar, 'Hold your head high, baby. Because when you walk with me, you're walking with Saracena's number one star!'

Although Jasper revelled in his role of Jester King, Stella was neither invited nor showed any inclination to play his Queen. She was neither the woman behind the man, nor the woman beside the man. In fact there was speculation, particularly among nubile females, as to whether she was still his woman in the biblical sense at all. Taciturn and razor-tongued by turns, Stella intimidated many and was an enigma to even more. The more outrageously Jasper frolicked, the tighter her barbed reserve. Her cool, almost contemptuous presence was that of an onlooker, a witness to the action rather than part of it. It took everybody by surprise therefore, when she suddenly stepped into the spotlight by announcing she was going to open a trattoria. It was generally assumed that Jasper was the inspiration behind such a brilliant idea. Which, in a way, he was. Having guzzled, gorged and partied his way through most of their savings, Stella was now faced with the need to generate an income.

Lengthy discussions immediately started about what to call the place. 'Colours', 'La Luna', 'Manhattan Sunrise' and, of course, 'J's', were all considered and rejected.

But in the end credit was given where credit was due. Long before it acquired its red and yellow painted sign, the trattoria was known simply as 'Stella's'.

Located in a vaulted and cavernous chamber inside the plunging feet-thick ramparts on the Saracena Mare side, Stella's was the first place in the history of the village to be established by an outsider. It was a Messori property like the Big House and it had also been empty for over twenty years. Older inhabitants remembered it serving variously as an olive press, council chamber and first-ever cinema. It took the whole winter to get it ready. A father and son team spent three months installing the two marble sinks and eight-ring gas cooker (a sprained shoulder, two funerals and a sciatica attack were variously blamed for the delays). Jasper and Ringo flooded the place twice attempting to plumb in a new toilet. In the end it was Billy's ex-lover, a plasterer by trade, who stepped in and finished the job. The rest of the work was done by friends staying at the Big House and occasional help from weekenders like us.

Or, rather, like me. After a week at his office Lorenzo refused to do anything more strenuous than sit around talking politics and drinking beer. For my part I pitched in to sand old paint from worn flagstones and slap whitewash over acres of rough plastered walls. It was great fun. The music blared and we were regularly refreshed with cocktails of white wine and *gassosa* (lemonade). While all this was going on Stella practised the art of cooking and at the end of the day a crowd of us sat around one of the long trestle tables to sample her efforts for free. One Saturday some friends of Jasper's arrived with a full-sized ping-pong table (it took hours to manoeuvre it through the narrow doorway and down the equally narrow stairs), after which ping-pong breaks punctuated the work routine. The children alternated being helpful with running wild. Of all of them Claudia was the least bother. Her new ambition was to be a cabaret artist and she kept herself amused by dancing provocatively on a table singing a tuneless version of a current pop song called something like 'Chirpy-chirpy-cheep-cheep'.

Louise arrived for her Easter holidays on 29 March. This happened to be both her eighteenth birthday and Stella's official opening night. Jasper considered this an auspicious coincidence and insisted she fulfil the functions of waitress and guest of honour concurrently. The menu started with a choice of mussel soup or pasta and ended with hash brownies. These were extremely potent and partly responsible for the rash of impromptu performances that followed. Notable was Ringo's expressive monologue in a language he claimed was medieval Bavarian. There was also the offering from Nicole, the heroin-addicted daughter of two French film stars, who had turned up in January and decided to stay. She sat on the ping-pong table and sang a sad song about unrequited love. It was fifteen verses long and ended with the spurned young woman committing suicide by drowning. She wept despairingly throughout our loud applause, then suddenly decided to whip off her blouse and expose her large-nippled breasts.

Nicole was tall, skinny and beautiful, with wild black hair and inch-long red lacquered nails. The children called her Cruella de Ville, fleeing in terror when she pounced on them waving her claws and clucking endearments. At some point during the evening she decided that Louise was her best friend and kept insisting she accept a fix as a birthday present. To escape her attentions Louise went home, leaving Nicole to lock herself in the toilet and shoot up alone. Perhaps she had trouble hitting a vein, but the result was that she splattered the freshly painted walls and ceiling with what looked like litres of her blood. And she would not be the last to do so. For the trattoria had been launched as it was to continue: an anarchic centre of seventies' freewheeling immorality.

Stella was assisted in the kitchen by Signora Assunta, a middle-aged widow with two children to support. Letizia, her daughter, was eleven and spent every afternoon there helping out. Her usual job was shelling shrimps, after which she did her school homework at one of the tables. She was a plain, very timid child who blushed furiously if anyone tried to talk to her. 'My treasure' Signora Assunta called her fondly. Her son Leonardo was 'my desperation'.

Leonardo was twenty. He dyed his hair blond and wore gaudy shirts unbuttoned to reveal a chest bristling with gold good-luck charms and religious medallions. Affectionate and dutiful, he called in to see Assunta most days, greeting her by kissing the top of her neatly braided head. Despite such charming displays of filial devotion, however, nobody could stand him. The reason for this was his driven determination to seduce whoever he was talking to. Regardless of whether the topic of conversation was cars, clothes or the latest political scandal, his body language was always the same. His torso writhed, his hands waved, eye contact was piercing and urgent, and the lower half of his face was one huge simpering smile. Furthermore, he put on the same performance regardless of the sex of the person he was addressing, which caused most people to dismiss him as an overtheatrical queen. But Brunetto insisted we had got it all wrong. In strict confidence he told me that although it was true Leonardo had been the lover of an elderly male hotel owner since the age of fourteen, he was not homosexual.

'You've got to understand that the family was left destitute when his father died,' he said. 'The hotel owner offered him pocket money, new shoes, a *motorino*... what could the boy do? It was a question of necessity, not preference. I know for a fact that he spends a large part of what the old man gives him on a whore called Maria Rosaria.'

The only person who didn't cringe at Leonardo's approach was Mob. Mob was a tall lanky Swede with hennaed hair, kohl-ringed eyes and an equally desperate need to make an impression. Claiming to be a doctor on a year's sabbatical from his Stockholm hospital, he arrived in the village offering to perform abortions for free (fortunately no woman was desperate or stupid enough to take up his offer). He then proceeded to work his way round the foreign community relating the story of his incestuous relationship with his mother; a relationship, he claimed, that was orchestrated by his stepfather when he was in his early teens.

When my turn came I was sitting on the low wall under the carob tree halfway up from the beach. It was early evening and I had stopped to watch the sea sink to invisibility in the deepening violet dusk. Ten yards below, a village woman foraged in scrubby vegetation stuffing handfuls of herbs and wild garlic into a frayed cloth bag slung across her chest. It was a rare moment of quiet contemplation and I was irritated by Mob's interruption.

I had already heard the story from other people, of course, and believed it no more than I believed he was a doctor. I did not tell him this, though. I listened with apparent attention, wondering at the conversational chattiness with which he recounted it. Thinking about it later, however, I conceded that it might have been true. And if so, could the fact they had both been victims of sexual abuse explain the empathetic understanding Mob and Leonardo appeared to share?

Be that as it may, they became friends. Cultural and language barriers did not exist for them. They hung around together, played billiards in the back room at Giovanni's and took trips down the coast on Leonardo's Vespa. On one occasion they disappeared to Naples for a week and returned unkempt, hung over, and with identical winged dragons tattooed on their biceps. After a month or so Mob's money had run out. He tried various income-generating ventures (making bead jewellery, for example, and offering cut-price Swedish conversation lessons) but nothing took off. Then one afternoon he called round at the trattoria and asked Stella if he could prepare his special meatballs for that night's menu. Stella, by now mightily fed up with cooking, agreed and crossed her fingers that they would be edible.

As it turned out they were more than edible. They were small, succulent, spicy and absolutely superb. So superb, in fact, that within minutes of eating them customers were clamouring for more.

'Mmmm… absolutely divine,' was Nicole's breathy verdict as she focused on Mob properly for the first time.

'Indeed,' agreed Nato. 'What else can you make?'

'What else?' replied Mob. 'Well, for a start my potato pancakes are the best in the world!'

And this was no idle boast, as he proved the following evening. He also produced a masterly fish soup and a flaky apricot tart that had people swooning. Stella was impressed. She immediately offered him a job. The money was negligible but he would be provided with food, drink and lodgings (which meant a room in the Big House with a mattress on the floor).

Mob became a contented and fulfilled man overnight. Not only were all his basic requirements taken care of, but every evening he was praised to the skies by grateful diners for his culinary skills. But although Mob and everybody else was happy, Signora Assunta was not. She complained that he got under her feet, that he was lazy and could not be bothered to wash the vegetables properly. She also objected to the fact that he always wore the same pair of red cotton trousers.

'It's unhygienic, Signora,' she complained to Stella. 'I mean, the man obviously doesn't wash his clothes.'

Stella and Signora Assunta had a good and harmonious relationship. In this instance, however, Stella was far too pleased with the present arrangement to respond to her gripes. And anyway, the real reason for Signora Assunta's hostility was that Mob was too much like her own son.

Another irritation for Signora Assunta was that her daughter, Letizia, adored him. This was curious given that Mob was not interested in children and made no effort to win her over. She loved helping him lay the tables and once, on arriving late and finding it had been done without her, she burst into tears. For his part, Mob rarely bothered to speak to her, possibly because she giggled herself silly every time he did. Unhappily,

Letizia's innocent infatuation was to have disastrous consequences. It cost Mob his friendship with Leonardo and, more importantly for the rest of us, the trattoria lost the best cook it would ever have.

Around five o'clock on a mid-August afternoon Mob left the trattoria to buy coarse-grained cooking salt. Stella and Signora Assunta were up to their elbows in the messy business of cleaning squid and did not notice that Letizia had slipped out after him. People reported seeing them walking hand-in-hand up the street before disappearing into the Big House. They stayed inside for roughly fifteen minutes and then returned to the trattoria. Letizia was doing her homework and Mob frying onions, garlic and rosemary in preparation for *Seppie in Umido* (squid casserole) when Leonardo burst in. '*T'ammazzo! Figlio di puttana!*' he screamed, throwing himself on Mob's neck. '*Hai rovinato mia sorella!*'

Mob found the accusation that he had 'ruined' Leonardo's sister incomprehensible. He tried to explain that he had gone to the Big House to collect his Zippo lighter. Letizia had insisted on tagging along so he had taken her with him. Once there he joined Ringo for a quick beer, leaving Letizia to entertain herself with Claudia's comics. But Leonardo was deaf to everything but the darkest implications of it all. Mob had taken Letizia, unchaperoned and in full view of the entire village, into a house that was now of the most notorious repute. His sister's character had been compromised forever and only a fool could think otherwise. Stella tried to reason with him to no avail. Even Signora Assunta (who hit Mob over the head with a broom) did not take such a cataclysmic view.

Mob left a few days later, boasting that he had been invited to stay with a countess friend at her villa on the island of

Ponza. Stella, reluctant to lose such a kitchen wizard, did her best to persuade him not to go. But Leonardo's anger continued unabated. You could sense it, knife-sharp, beneath the veneer of his determined charm.

I was in the kitchen one afternoon when Leonardo arrived to escort his sister home, something he now did every day. Stella suggested that it hardly seemed necessary as they only lived fifty yards away. 'One has to be careful with girls,' he retorted bitterly. 'I want Letizia to marry well. I'm only sorry that I'm a poor man and haven't the money to keep her in a convent school until she's eighteen.'

'He could start by getting up in the morning and looking for a job,' Signora Assunta commented sourly after they had gone. 'He's waiting for Jesus to take pity on him and change his fortune.'

And maybe that's just what happened because a few months later Leonardo won a considerable sum on the national lottery. Nobody in Torre Saracena had ever been so lucky and the entire village packed into the church to hear the priest mention it in his sermon. Stella called me in Rome with the details. Leonardo was the man of the moment, she said, the living proof that it was possible for dreams to come true. He had exchanged his Vespa for an Alfa Romeo, bought his mother a full-length mink coat, and was planning to open a bar with pinball machines and a jukebox in Saracena Mare. Only Letizia, it seemed, wasn't rejoicing – and who could blame her? To safeguard her virtue Leonardo had packed her off to spend the next seven years at a convent school in the far north of Italy.

Seppie in umido

A phobic dislike of minced beef meant I never tried Mob's meatballs. I was so mad about his potato pancakes, however, that I spent an afternoon as his kitchen skivvy in order to learn how to make them. My other favourite dish of his was cuttlefish stewed with white wine and tomatoes.

Feeds 4

1 kg (2 lb 3 oz) seppie (cuttlefish, alternatively squid), prepared and cleaned
200 g (7 oz) tomato sauce (home-made is better)
1 onion, chopped
2 cloves garlic, chopped
Small bunch of fresh parsley
Extra virgin olive oil
½ large glass white wine
2 tinned anchovies, chopped

Clean and wash the *seppie* and cut them roughly into strips. Lightly fry the onion and garlic with the anchovies. Add the ½ glass of wine. Let it reduce a little, then add the tomato sauce and the *seppie* and season to taste. Place on a low heat and simmer covered for about 30–35 minutes. The liquid should be thick and jammy. Stir in the freshly chopped parsley and serve.

Chapter Six

THE YEAR BRUNETTO IL PICCOLO FELL IN LOVE

The summer season proper started after the schools closed for the holidays in June. Torre Saracena aficionados arrived from America and Europe to join those of us who now came regularly from all over Italy. For several years there was even an Eskimo devotee, a girl called Taki, who made the yearly pilgrimage all the way from northern Canada. By July the population had more than tripled, creating serious problems for the ancient sewage system. The apartments with purple bougainvillea climbing the walls, terraced gardens and balconies overlooking the sea were quickly snapped up by the rich. The less affluent rented dark, airless grottoes with walls that dripped condensation and turned clothes and bedlinen green with creeping mould. The willingness – ardour even – with which visitors occupied what had for centuries accommodated mules or vats of oil and wine confirmed the Saracenesi's belief that foreigners were quite mad. It wasn't a wholly unwelcome madness, however. People began looking at their cellar space with new eyes and learned to describe cracked stone floors and rotting beams with the exotic term *caratteristico*. Suddenly opportunities for financial gain were wondrously expanded. Even those who had never thought they had anything of worth to sell were now poised to jump on the tourist bandwagon.

Brunetto il Piccolo, one of the first to take advantage of the new opportunities, was the most prominent presence on the apartment letting front. His friendship with many of the newcomers and his skill as a property go-between had taken him from a lifetime's penury to a strutting new affluence. In the early years, except on the occasion of his aunt's funeral, I never saw him in anything other than a faded blue T-shirt and limp pink shorts. Now he was an immaculate and stylish dresser, regularly visiting the barber's in the main street for a shave, trim and manicure. It was the accessories, however, that defined his new style: the row of red and blue biros bristling in his shirt pocket, the green tinted sunglasses, the carton of contraband Marlboros cradled under one arm and, most importantly, the brown leather handbag.

This prized possession – of the type made popular when Italian men's trousers got too tight for anything larger than a slimline Zippo – accompanied him everywhere. Signora Lucia, who had no extra space to let and had conducted a long and bitter feud with Brunetto's mother, was one of the many not impressed by the transformation.

'Once a *cafone*, always a *cafone*,' she commented contemptuously as we watched him saunter past our communal stairs. 'You can put a pig in a silk suit but a pig he stays.'

Brunetto conducted his business in the Piazza, positioned halfway between Giovanni's bar and the *tabaccheria*. For a large part of each day he stood in the same spot, receiving a steady stream of would-be lessors and lessees. His air of solemn dignity and the impression he gave that the solution to any problem was in his hands gave him the aura of a diminutive Godfather. His main rival, also called Brunetto, had his pitch on the opposite side of the Piazza. Tall, stooped, crafty and in his sixties, he lost more than one commission by lunging at the breasts of foreign female clients. Brunetto il Piccolo, on the other hand, was far too astute to endanger his livelihood by such behaviour. Not that he was free from temptation. Sex, as I well knew from our many conversations, was a topic never far from his mind.

During the first year of our friendship, sitting in my kitchen chatting after he brought Marcello back from the cinema, the subject of women and the bitter humiliations inflicted by the local girls was something he returned to again and again. On one occasion, talking about Silvia, a girl on whom he'd had a passionate crush at 14, he even cried. According to Brunetto, Silvia had loved him too. Her father, however, who noticed the glances they exchanged, had threatened to disembowel Brunetto if he so much as looked in her direction again.

Brunetto's amorous problems were due to his occupying the lowest rung in a desperately poor village. His father eked out a miserable living as a fisherman. The family had no land, no prospects, and seven of them shared a two-room apartment. His older brother was epileptic, indicating bad blood perpetuated by intermarriage and confirmed by the fact that they were all extremely short (that intermarriage and its consequences were common to the entire village was not taken into consideration). His one romantic success was a furtive affair with a much older widow. But she quickly dropped him when a man who had been an immigrant for twenty years in Marseilles returned with a suitcase full of savings and started courting her.

Unmarried sex, particularly in the south of Italy, had never been easy. Men with good looks and charm took advantage of the summer influx of females who tripped off planes and tourist buses hot for suntans and Latin romance. The less fortunate men took their libidinous needs to whores. What little money Brunetto il Piccolo managed to save was spent on hookers picked up in bars like the Splash B-Way in the nearby port town or on the fat, ageing women who warmed their bellies and billowing thighs at carefully tended bonfires strung out along the main road to Naples. For these occasions he borrowed one of the small, battered Vespa trucks used by local tomato growers, cruising slowly past tough-faced matrons who lazily lifted their skirts at approaching headlights to tempt prospective clients with a flash of their goods.

Because of his lack of money it was these *Belle di Notte* rather than the more expensive Splash B-Way girls that most often got his custom. Their business was mainly with the long-distance lorry drivers and travelling salesmen who were serviced for as little as 500 lire. As Brunetto was always at pains to point out, however, the size of the fee was not reflected in their skill – especially where a certain Concetta 'The Tongue' was concerned. He drew an analogy with roadside trattorias.

'If you see a line of trucks outside, you take that as a sign the food's good, don't you?' he said. 'Well, it's the same with whores. Truckers only go where there's value for money.'

Until Torre Saracena's Big Bang, Brunetto il Piccolo had resigned himself to making do with whores forever. But as an up-and-coming entrepreneur his matrimonial prospects were no longer so bleak. Although his emergence as a central player in Saracena's new order was regarded with the same amazement as the upgrading of dank cellars, several shrewd matriarchs were sizing him up as a possible husband for their plainer daughters.

But Brunetto's requirements had changed along with his circumstances. The satisfaction he now anticipated from marriage had as much to do with revenge as it did with anything else. With his new and inflated self-regard he aspired to a dazzling match that would be a salve to his wounds and a lesson to all those who had been stupid enough to reject him in the past. He now dismissed local girls as '*troppo semplice e ignorante*'. The wife he fantasised about would be 'a Rose, a Diamond, a Shining Star.'

One evening in early July – after promising faithfully to produce a cheap, honest plumber to deal with the leak under our bathroom floor – he returned to the subject yet again. 'Nothing less than the best will do for me,' he insisted, thumping his handbag for emphasis. I was already irritable because of the leak and his arrogance annoyed me further.

'With that attitude sweet nothing is what you'll get!' I snapped.

But I was wrong. The following morning two Germans arrived in a taxi from the station. And one of them was the dream woman Brunetto il Piccolo had been waiting for.

Helga Schultz was a very short blonde in her late thirties with knowing grey eyes and a very generously proportioned backside. It was this part of her anatomy, shown to its best advantage in tight white trousers, that Brunetto first noticed when she approached him for accommodation. The elderly man with her was in a state of near collapse from the heat. Leaving her to sort out the accommodation, he disappeared into Giovanni's to restore himself with several beers. (He was later explained away as her rich industrialist uncle.)

The transaction, like all Brunetto's transactions with foreigners, was conducted mostly in sign language. What made it different this time was the unmistakably encouraging nature of her body language. The flames of passion and love, Brunetto told everyone later, were ignited there and then. From that moment on anybody needing his services had a hard time finding him. Professional obligations took second place to the demands of his first-ever proper courtship.

Every morning at 8.45 the three of them went down to the beach; Helga supporting the old man on her sturdy arm, Brunetto staggering behind under the weight of their collective beach paraphernalia. With uncle comfortably parked in the shade of one of Leone's umbrellas, Brunetto inflated the rubber dinghy (borrowed from a nine-year-old nephew) and paddled his sweetheart fifteen yards or so out to sea. For a blissful couple of hours they bobbed about on the gentle waves, eyes locked, hands entwined, totally oblivious to shrieking children or the curious, amused attention they attracted.

Communication in those early days posed no problem: a pocket German/Italian dictionary more than satisfied their verbal needs. And the success of their physical communion was such that an aura of charged contentment surrounded them at all times. Both blond, five foot and a bit, they looked as though they'd been especially crafted for each other, like bookends or matching jigsaw pieces. In the evening they joined the promenade of people strolling back and forth from the Piazza to the bridge, arms around each other's waists, eating ice cream and graciously acknowledging greetings from Brunetto's many friends and acquaintances. Sometimes he took her for a ride on the back of the noisy second-hand *motorino* to which he had hung a precariously fixed sign advertising his professional calling. The uncle was rarely seen and after two weeks he returned alone to Germany. A week or so later Helga and Brunetto il Piccolo announced they were going to marry.

Brunetto did his best to ensure his romance inspired the envy and admiration he hungered for. He boasted about Helga's finesse, how sophisticated and well travelled she was, and about the big factory uncle owned on the outskirts of Essen. He carried around a photograph of her leaning against a Mercedes-Benz and another of her wearing a sequinned evening dress taken in a smart nightclub. But the response of the village was grudging. The general consensus was that she was 'shop-soiled' and 'second-hand goods'. Or, as Signora Lucia put it, 'There's a worm in that apple somewhere.'

The 'worm' arrived at the end of October carrying a single shabby suitcase secured with a raincoat belt. She was a lanky 15-year-old introduced as Helga's little sister, Greta. Helga and Brunetto il Piccolo were now married and comfortably ensconced in the bottom half of one of the new villas built at the entrance to the village. With the end of the season and the departure of the summer people he was free to devote himself exclusively to his wife. Every morning they set off hand in hand to do the shopping, Helga pointing and Brunetto teaching her the Italian name of the selected food item. And every evening they continued to promenade slowly up and down between the Piazza and the bridge. But although they kept their smiles bright and their arms locked around each other's waists, it was clear that the sullen adolescent trailing behind them was casting a dark shadow onto their heaven.

Brunetto had not fulfilled his promise to find me an honest and reliable plumber. In mid-November he phoned Rome to say that the leak was worse and water was pouring into the bedroom of the old woman below. Exasperated, I arranged for my mother-in-law to look after the boys and left for Torre Saracena, prepared to stay for at least a week.

It was unseasonably warm, almost summer-like. Alighting from the midday bus and seeing the sun glittering on a satin-smooth sea, I was tempted to forget the problem and go for a swim. Instead I dumped my bag in the flat and went to the bar for advice from Pina as to what could be done.

The reason I was having a problem getting a plumber was because I bought vegetables from Signora Rosalba's stall and not from Signora Annamaria. Signora Annamaria was married to the only plumber in the village and lived in the apartment below my mother's. Furthermore, it was on her mother's head that my bathroom was leaking. Despite the fact that she and her family were suffering the consequences, Annamaria refused to allow her husband to come and fix it. Not only was I her rival's customer, but I had once accused her of overcharging. I had rowed with her, reasoned with her, begged her. All to no avail. We were locked into a familiar village stalemate.

Pina did not need me to explain the situation. As with all village gossip, she knew it already. 'You have two options,' she said. 'Either you get a plumber from Matia, or you get somebody with influence to approach Signora Annamaria on your behalf. There's no other way.'

I carried my *latte macchiato* outside. Being off-season there were no tables, so I sat on the broad stone ledge running along the wall coasting the steps. I racked my brains trying to think of a possible mediator but to no avail. I was not on familiar terms with either the priest, the mayor or the head of the elementary school. I was quite friendly with Signora Annamaria's second cousin, Rita, but as they had quarrelled over property and hardly spoke there was nothing to be gained there. As it happened, however, fate decided to intervene and the problem was resolved without my needing a mediator after all.

In the two short months she had been in the village, Greta had done much to tarnish Brunetto's carefully nurtured image. She hung about the Piazza looking pinched, defiant and neglected, soliciting cigarettes or a few lire from any man or foreign woman who happened to glance her way. Joining me on the wall, she immediately indicated she wanted one of my Nazionales. After lighting up she exhaled noisily and muttered something in German that sounded like 'Torre Saracena stinks.' She said it with such venom that I burst out laughing. My reaction took her by surprise.

'American, ya?'

'English.'

'Ah! Beatles! Rolling Stones! You like?'

I nodded, adding, 'And you'll like Torre Saracena better when spring comes. There are lots more people. Young people, your age.'

'You crazy?' She glared and tapped her forehead with a finger. 'I don't stay in this stinkhole for spring with them two stinking crazy shits! I split!'

I felt sorry for her and sorry for Brunetto il Piccolo, too. A ready-made teenage rebellion was never part of his plans.

The following day was spent asking everyone and anyone if they knew of a plumber who could come to my rescue. I was told long stories of outrageous overcharging, work left unfinished and old parts sneaked in instead of new. Salvatore the *Pasticiere* said if I had come to him a week earlier he could have helped me but the man in question, who lived in Matia, had suffered a sudden heart attack and died. By then I was thoroughly fed up. It was late afternoon and I decided to cheer myself up with a walk on the beach and a bowl of Leone's mother's mussel soup.

For me, mussel soup made in Torre Saracena – although the recipe is simple and by no means unique – tastes better than any mussel soup anywhere else in the world. It is the village's one great culinary achievement. The fresh mussels are stewed with white wine, garlic and parsley and the resulting juice, sopped up with crusty hunks of pungent *cassareccio* bread, is pure ambrosia. Consequently, it was with salivating anticipation that I hurried down the broad stone-stepped path to the beach. The sun was setting when I arrived at Leone's and the place appeared deserted. Nosing around, however, I soon came across the mother dozing in a deckchair behind the kitchen. She awoke immediately and declared herself happy to serve me a plate of the mussels she had cooked that day for lunch.

I went to sit on the wooden veranda to wait. The sea was rose-tinted and the beach an empty silken sweep of sand. The spacious silence broken only by the gentle lapping of waves was so numinously awesome I found myself holding my breath.

'It's so beautiful,' I murmured reverently when Leone's mother brought me the soup.

'*E bella, si*,' the old lady replied, smiling toothlessly. 'And once upon a time it was always like this. No umbrellas, no jukebox, no noise.'

It was dark when we said goodbye but I still wasn't ready to go home. Slipping off my shoes I continued barefoot toward the promontory at the far end of the beach. Suddenly the silence was shattered by a drunken voice booming from behind a clump of bushes.

'Oh, fuck her,' a man with a harsh American accent exclaimed. 'She's just a pain in the ass.'

Drawing closer I saw three marines from the American naval base sprawled around a crackling driftwood fire, bottles of wine and leftovers from a picnic littered everywhere. There were two young girls with them. The girl wearing just her knickers was Greta. She giggled happily while one man pawed her breasts and another kissed her. The other, small and slight with a waist-length plait of dark hair, was struggling to escape from a slobbering brute. It was Gianna, Signora Annamaria's 13-year-old daughter.

My arrival broke up the party. I informed the men that the girls were underage, which meant if they weren't court-martialled they would certainly be lynched. I also added that I was the wife of Sir Reginald Williams, the British Ambassador to Rome. This little lie had great effect and they couldn't get away fast enough. Greta was furious. She yanked on a T-shirt and ran off swearing at me in German and English for spoiling her fun.

I put my arms around Gianna and held her until she stopped shaking. Then, with her clinging to my hand, we started the long climb back up to the village.

'Don't tell my parents,' she begged repeatedly. 'They'll kill me.'

I said I wouldn't if she faithfully promised to keep away from Greta in future. But how she was going to explain the torn blouse and the scratches on her neck and arms, I didn't know.

Signora Annamaria, informed by at least ten people that her daughter had gone down to the beach with Greta, was waiting in a smouldering lather at the top of the steps. When we appeared she immediately seized Gianna by the hair and began walloping her. Then she dragged her off screaming about worse retributions to follow.

The shouting and crying from their apartment went on late into the night. At some point Gianna must have confessed everything – including the part I had played – because at half past seven the next morning the plumber husband was at my door. Neither of us made any reference to the recent dramatic events. All he said was that he now found he had time to attend to my problem. After a quick inspection he explained that the leak came from one of the pipes feeding the shower and to get at it some of the floor tiles would have to be broken. But I was not to worry. It would not be expensive and the job would be finished in a couple of days.

Later that morning I shopped at Signora Rosalba's as usual, but I bought a kilo of tomatoes from Signora Annamaria's stall as well.

'Ah, children are such a trial, isn't that so, Signora?' she said, picking out the best tomatoes for me. 'And boys can be as much of a worry in their way as girls.'

'You're so right,' I replied. 'And my boys get up to so much mischief I'm worried most of the time.'

We shook our heads, shrugged heavily and gave a couple of long weary sighs. I was given not only a discount but also two lemons, an onion and a fist-sized bunch of basil for free. Hostilities had ceased – although problems with our bathroom plumbing were to prove never-ending.

I didn't see Greta for the rest of my stay but Signora Lucia gave me a vivid account of the scene that occurred a few weeks later. A small travelling circus arrived in the village and a clown with a performing monkey turned up in the Piazza to advertise the evening's performance. Among the crowd that gathered to watch its antics was Brunetto il Piccolo with Helga and Greta. The clown had a megaphone which he put down for a moment in order to better encourage the animal to walk on its hands. Suddenly Greta snatched it up and put it to her lips. Signora Lucia claimed her voice carried for miles.

'She stinking liar!' she bellowed pointing at a horror-struck Helga. 'Not sister – mother! *Madre!* My stupid idiot mother, you hear!'

Signora Lucia told me this while she prepared lunch in the cubbyhole kitchen hung with bunches of dried herbs and black iron cooking pots.

'You see, I was right,' she declared with satisfaction. 'I said there was a worm in that apple somewhere.'

Cozze alla marinara

Leone's mother was in her mid-fifties but looked twenty years older. Lines were etched deep into her leathery skin and what remained of her teeth were yellowed stumps. She was a shy woman, monosyllabic when her husband was around. On the occasion I found Greta and Gianna with the American sailors, however, he was nowhere to be seen. Neither were the rest of her family and their absence made her positively chatty. She was gratified at my praise of her mussel soup and eager to share the recipe.

Feeds 4

*1.5 kg (3 lb 5 oz) mussels
3–4 cloves of garlic, crushed flat
1 small piece fresh red chilli pepper
Handful finely-chopped parsley
4 tbsp extra virgin olive oil
Bottle dry white wine
Pepper
Crusty bread to serve*

Leave the mussels purging in lightly salted water for a couple of hours. Throw away any that have opened, rinse the rest. Put the mussels in a wide pan or baking tray with the crushed garlic, hot red pepper, and oil. Add the wine. Cover with a lid and cook over a lively heat. When the mussels have opened sprinkle with parsley, season with pepper, and serve with robust hunks of crusty bread. Don't eat any that haven't opened.

Chapter Seven

THE CHILDREN'S WARS

One late June afternoon I came up from the beach to be confronted by a bizarre sight. Marcello and his best friend Sandro were lounging toughly on the steps of my mother's flat with sanitary towels stretched across their faces. The end loops had been hooked around their ears and the gauze padding carefully positioned to cover the area from nose to chin. I hurriedly whipped the things off, explaining that although they might look like gas masks, their actual function was to be worn inside ladies' knickers. This mortifying information was received with choking, groaning and horrified slapping of foreheads. I told them not to worry, however, as nobody seemed to have even registered their presence, which a rapid glance around the Piazza confirmed. But it was a close shave and the awareness of the potential damage to their dignity meant it was a good couple of hours before they recovered.

Privately I found the whole thing endearingly funny and also hoped it would stop them plundering my stuff for props for their games (metal belts were a favourite, as was a brocade waistcoat that frequently doubled as a bulletproof vest). It was only later that I discovered that the 'gas masks' were part of something quite serious. Marcello and Sandro were psyching themselves up for a confrontation they had been tensely anticipating since our arrival for the summer a few days earlier.

Children's wars had always been a part of Torre Saracena life. The Via Ripa gang, for example, was a historic antagonist of the gang that congregated near the old church; the Belvedere lot were against those from Saracena Mare, and so on. Marcello had only been in the village a few hours the year of our first summer when he was initiated into this pre-teen reality. During an exploratory tour of Torre Saracena's narrow passageways he was jumped on, beaten up and made to understand that his only allies would be among outsiders like himself. But it was not until a couple of years later – when he was eight and had an established group of friends – that hostilities were properly formalised.

From then on the map of Torre Saracena was criss-crossed with no-go areas and safe havens. Marcello's gang claimed the Piazza, the Ponte and the New Piazza. Domenico, a year or so older and leader of the biggest Torre Saracena gang, controlled Via S. Leone, the piazzetta where Califano the tailor had his vaulted burrow of a shop, and all the interlinking alleyways. On one occasion Marcello and Sandro were under siege in our Via S. Leone room for several hours. After long negotiations – conducted from the safety of the balcony – it was agreed that a model London bus (a much-prized present from my mother) would buy their safe conduct. As soon as they came out, however, the bus was snatched and they were set upon with sticks and sand-filled plastic truncheons.

Their response was to convene an emergency war council to discuss punitive retaliation. About eight boys turned up and a few girls, too. After much debate it was decided to formally challenge 'the treacherous sneaks' to a battle in the big car park behind the Town Hall, a traditional fighting place for children and adults alike as it wasn't overlooked. The challenge was eagerly accepted and the next two days were dedicated to the preparations. This didn't mean strategy or tactics. It meant devising and constructing an array of nasty weapons. These included the time-honoured catapult, bows for the shooting of umbrella-spoke arrows, and a crossbow made from planks of wood and thick elastic bands which, when released by a clothes' peg secured to the plank, fired bent nails.

The battle was arranged for after lunch. Everyone agreed on this because the only guaranteed 'parent-safe' time was between 2 and 4 p.m. At that hour *forestieri* genitors were frying on the beach, while those of the Saracenesi children were taking their afternoon siesta. And so it was that, free from parental control and with the sun at its blazing zenith, the tribal ritual took place.

Hostilities opened with the opposing factions facing each other at a sensibly cautious distance across a flinty expanse of sand and gravel. For twenty minutes or so the warriors screamed insults, threw stones and fired an assortment of missiles from their carefully constructed weapons. It was an elaborate and highly enjoyable form of chest-beating which prepared them for the second phase: hand-to-hand combat.

Until then, apart from the odd puncture wound inflicted by an umbrella spoke, no real injuries were sustained. This changed when proper fighting started. Noses were bloodied, faces clawed, ribs and shins kicked and bruised. The *forestieri* gang were advantaged in that they were accompanied by their posse of loud-mouthed female supporters. Claudia, Tammy, Fausta and the two Patrizias (one fat and one thin) ran up and down the sidelines egging their warriors on with raucous shrieks. They kept this up until both sides, trumpeting loudly about the performance of their troops on the field, decided they had had enough and began retreating. Each side claimed absolute victory. Defeat only ever happened to the adversary.

The battle Marcello and Sandro were now anticipating was different in that the cause for it had been made several months earlier in Rome. One afternoon, when Marcello should have been at school for remedial maths coaching, he hooked up with Sandro and went to the zoo. While queuing at the kiosk to buy fish for the barking patriarch who ruled the seal pool, they suddenly spotted Domenico and his class marching in regimented, spic and span pairs around the other side. Surprise and delight knew no bounds. With three hatchet-faced teachers supervising the column, their antagonists had been delivered into their malicious hands as powerless as sacrificial lambs. It was more than they could have dreamed of: a gift-wrapped opportunity that they were determined to exploit to the full.

From seal pool to ape house, from ape house to elephant pit, they dogged the Saracenesi's footsteps, keeping up a non-stop torrent of taunts and jeers. And flaunting their own freedom in a manner to make their rivals' lack of it even more painful, they climbéd poles, swung on bars, leapfrogged benches and generally cavorted like a pair of malevolent demons. The impotent fury of their humiliated enemies gave them enormous satisfaction and they continued the gleeful torture to the bitter end. As the Saracenesi were being herded back onto their hired bus, Domenico could contain himself no more.

'Just you wait till the summer!' he yelled, baring his teeth. 'We'll get you for this!'

The day of the sanitary towel gas masks was the first day Marcello and Sandro had ventured into the Piazza alone. Since our arrival four days earlier, they had spent all the time they were not with me on the beach cowering indoors. Their fear of what awaited them was not helped by what happened to Davide and the Italo-German twins, Michele and Roberto, when they sneaked off to the ruined tower on the Belvedere to smoke cigarettes filched from Davide's psychiatrist father.

Just as they were lighting up, Domenico's gang burst in wielding whips of knotted electric flex. After confiscating the cigarettes, the three were lined up against the wall and Domenico told them that smoking was a terrible sin which merited the most severe of punishments. He then ordered his grinning henchmen to flog the offenders to death.

At their tearful pleas for mercy, however, he agreed to commute the sentence to ten sharp strokes on each offending bum. At this point Michele and Roberto pointed out that if their mother found so much as a mark on either of them all hell would break loose. To Saracenesi and *forestieri* children alike, mothers ranked top among life's awesome forces. And the twins' mother – a steely-eyed Valkyrie of towering presence – was more awesome than most. Taking this into consideration, Domenico made a further reluctant concession. T-shirts, he said, could be taken off and stuffed inside trousers as protective pads.

By ducking, diving and extreme circumspection, Sandro and Marcello managed to defer their day of reckoning for almost two weeks. (Although Marcello was ambushed on the beach by Leone's drummer brother, Gino, and two others in retaliation for an unconnected offence. After marching him to the field at the back of the kitchen, they tied him to an olive tree and lit a fire under his feet. His rubber flip-flops had all but melted by the time he was rescued.) In the end they were caught because, despite the danger the gang posed, they could not resist the lure of the travelling circus when it rolled into town.

The circus was a family-run affair of unique charm. Father was ringmaster, fire-eater and animal trainer. Mother, a plump figure in a swimsuit sewn with sequins, wobbled precariously along a low tightrope holding a cane. She also did lumbering somersaults and the splits. Two daughters aged about seven and nine, also wearing sequinned swimsuits, performed a hit-and-miss juggling act with coloured hoops. The son, a good-looking lad of about seventeen, did card tricks and plucked hundred lire coins from ears, beards and gentlemen's breast pockets. There were also two clowns, a monkey, three or four performing dogs and an old, bored-looking bear who waved a weary paw when asked to say '*ciao*'.

Marcello and Sandro had pinned their hopes on being protected by the crowd. No way. They were ambushed as they tried to steal off at the end of the performance and were frogmarched to scrubland at the rear of the patched and faded Big Top.

'*Scapigliato!*' (dialect for long unruly hair, and the local kids' nickname for Marcello) Domenico hissed. 'Now you're going to die. You and that stinking *capa di culo* [bumhead] with you!'

His gang responded to this with a baying chorus of approval. The moment of their long-awaited revenge had finally come. The tables were turned. Now it was Marcello and Sandro's turn to suffer.

The Saracenesi gang closed in, teeth and eyes glinting ferociously in the moonlight. '*Memma che ditt che siete!*' ('Mamma, what little pricks you are!') they jeered, beating the ground with their sticks. 'Look at them pissing their pants! What's the matter *guaglioni*? Swallowed your tongues?'

Sandro and Marcello knew they had earned this fate and there was no point in trying to negotiate. They steeled themselves to endure whatever was coming with as much fortitude as possible. And to a certain extent they succeeded. For despite being prodded, whacked, mocked, spat on and finally debagged, neither of them actually broke down and cried. But all that was just for starters. Triumphantly hoisting Marcello's jeans on the top of his stick, Domenico announced that the 'proper battle' was still to come and it would take place in the car park as usual.

The night before the 'proper battle' a spaghetti Western was shown at the open-air cinema next to the school. It climaxed with the hero and the evil leader of a bunch of outlaws slugging it out on the empty main street of a frontier town. All the children loved spaghetti Westerns, but it was the swaggering fearlessness of stars like Bud Spencer and Terence Hill that the boys particularly identified with. Inspired by the film, Domenico sent Marcello a message proposing one-to-one combat instead of the usual all-out fray. Marcello immediately agreed. It was not only that the vision of himself as a vanquishing hero was irresistible, it also accorded with his maturing ideas of how rival gang leaders should behave.

Marcello and Domenico did not really dislike each other. In fact, they regarded each other with the respect alleged to exist between generals of opposing armies. Both had developed a code of honour (of sorts) accepting that a certain moral responsibility went with authority. When they met to discuss details, therefore, they agreed there would be no eye gouging, nose biting, ear twisting or kicks to the groin. They were going to set an example and fight clean.

The afternoon of the encounter was particularly hot. The handful of vehicles in the car park shimmered incandescently. The rival gang members squatted opposite each other in a large circle, eating dried pumpkinseeds and spitting the chewed husks into the air. Meanwhile the combatants flexed muscles, jogged up and down and generally put a lot of effort into looking fierce. Claudia, Tammy and the other girls were ranged in a high-spirited line along a wall. Losing patience with the prolonged macho posturing, they began clamouring for action. Several of the boys agreed. 'That's right. What are we waiting for? Let's get on with it, no?'

Domenico ceremoniously removed his watch and handed it to his second-in-command for safekeeping. Marcello – much aggrieved that he had no watch himself – borrowed Claudia's beaded sash and tied it around his matted mop of sun-bleached curls like a bandanna. Then, heads lowered, they rushed at each other.

Audience participation was as important as the action. Each swinging punch, each heaving, bone-crunching clinch was accompanied by cheers, boos, stamping and ear-piercing whistles. Domenico had weight on his side, Marcello agility. The fight lasted for about half an hour and concluded when both parties were too exhausted to go on. Marcello had a split lip, Domenico cuts and grazes, but there was no outright winner. Despite this, and despite the fact that nobody got to make or shoot weapons, the event was voted a complete success. So much so, in fact, that many future disputes were settled in the same way.

Marcello's involvement in gang warfare ceased around the age of twelve when girls became an increasingly absorbing interest. By then the make-up of the gangs had also changed. Village children were now allowed to play on the beach with the result that new, cross-pollinated alliances were formed. When Luca joined the *forestieri* gang, for example, it was perfectly natural that several of his village friends should join with him. And the summer Domenico's younger brother, Riccardo, stepped into his shoes, he appointed a freckle-faced American boy with glasses and sticky-up red hair as his second-in-command.

For Marcello and Domenico, however, friendship only arrived in their mid-teens when they found themselves face-to-face on the bridge wearing the same Persol 649 sunglasses (Persol 649s being the coolest and most ardently desired style accessory of that summer). Anyone who had a pair was acknowledged as a kindred spirit and part of a sophisticated elite. So there and then they formally shook hands and put the years of antagonism behind them. After that they met often (wearing their Persols, of course) to smoke Marlboros – a habit Domenico unfortunately no longer considered a sin – and reminisce nostalgically about the battles of the 'good old days' like campaign veterans.

'It's not the same now,' Marcello would say. 'Not the weapons, the tactics, the spirit – nothing.'

And, shaking his head sadly, Domenico would agree.

Frappe

Salvatore, owner of the *pasticcieria* producing the *cornetti* with napalm-hot jam, was a young man from the nearby port town. He was married to a local girl and they had a young son. His workday started at 5 a.m., so if we needed an early start he obligingly knocked on our door (for us Torre Saracena was a strictly alarm-clock-free zone). He had a soft spot for Marcello, Luca, and Marcello's friend, Sandro, often presenting them with a bag of unsold cakes at the end of the day. Of all the wonderful things he produced, *frappe* (fried cookies made especially for Carnival) were their favourite.

Makes a satisfying pile

350 g (12 oz) finely-sifted plain flour
50 g (2 oz) creamed butter
1 pinch of salt
2 large eggs
2 tbsp icing sugar flavoured with 2 drops vanilla extract
Oil or lard for frying

Knead quickly the flour, butter, salt and eggs. When dough is smooth and silky, wrap in a napkin and let rest for 1 hour. Divide the dough, roll it two or three times into a sheet about 3 mm (0.12 in) thick, then cut into triangles, rectangles or ribbons. Fry the pieces in the hot fat, drain onto kitchen paper, sprinkle with the vanilla-flavoured icing sugar and serve.

Chapter Eight

MICIA

The Saturday market in Torre Saracena was where I first saw women buying live chickens for the table. It was both fascinating and repellent and reminded me that *pollo arrosto* started, not neatly trussed on a supermarket shelf, but with primitive, bloody sacrifice. The scraggy, squalling birds with their crushed, dirty feathers and frantic bobbing heads were either squashed into small wire cages or tethered tightly to a table leg. The seller was a huge red-haired man who had once been a sailor and always wore a battered old yachting cap. For each potential customer he seized a chicken with a great meaty paw and held it upside down for inspection. This took time as sharp-eyed women checked out its health, age, fleshiness and size. According to Signora Lucia, a good hen with a clutch of unlaid eggs in its ovaries was the best buy.

'It's tough and takes long cooking,' she said. 'But the broth you get is rich and yellow and full of flavour. And if you're ailing, *figlia mia*, it'll build you up like nothing else will.'

Birds were purchased two, three, even four at a time. They were carried home by their clawed feet, heads skimming the slippery smooth paving stones, terrified wings beating a helpless protest against the robust implacability of their captor's broad thighs. And it was usually in the kitchen, with the children looking on, that they squawked their last. Pinioned between strong knees, necks were wrung, feathers plucked, and warm innards spilled in sanguinary clumps on marble-topped tables.

The Saracenesi, like all Italian peasants, were unsentimental about animals. They either served a useful purpose or they were eaten. The idea of keeping pets – walking around trailing an over-fed dog on a lead, for example – was an absurd and alien concept. This attitude was reflected in the village's relationship with its large colony of feral cats. Tolerated only because they kept the teeming rat population under control, these wild, sharp-faced, grey and white tabbies received few favours and trusted nobody. (The tender-hearted butcher was the one notable exception. At 5 a.m. the little piazzetta next to his shop was crowded with cats waiting for the scraps he threw them.)

During the day they lurked in dark storerooms or crouched warily on high ledges and in the many dips and crevices of the interconnecting rooftops. At night they foraged for food among the bulging plastic rubbish bags placed out in the street for collection. It was a perilous existence and many succumbed to disease and deliberate poisoning. It was also said that certain Saracenesi (Tullio on the beach among them) were dedicated consumers of cat stew. Of all these dangers, however, it was the village boys these beleaguered felines feared the most. With a savagery rooted in centuries of poverty and isolation, the trapping and persecution of cats (and stray dogs) was a favourite diversion.

Girls and boys played different games in Torre Saracena. Active cruelty to animals was an exclusively male pursuit. Although the adults did not condone it, they shrugged it off as just one of the many unruly aspects of boyhood. Brunetto il Piccolo, for example – while insisting that he himself had never indulged in it – put animal torture on a par with laughing in church, telling dirty jokes or smoking dried weeds in scraps of rolled up newspaper.

My introduction to this ferocious reality occurred during my first summer when I followed the dirt track through the back-lying hills to fill two large plastic water containers at a freshwater spring. In the first tuck of the road, on the scrubbed step of a small stone farmhouse, a couple of six-year-olds were crouched in intense concentration. Pink and red geraniums planted in an assortment of tin cans spilled in luxurious profusion from the windowsill above their heads. Behind, in the recessed doorway, an immaculate white net curtain fluttered gently in the breeze, giving an occasional glimpse of the cool, shuttered interior beyond. At the side of the house a young girl in a faded print dress was carrying wine and bread to the table set beneath gnarled old cherry trees.

It was a scene of such idyllic perfection that it stopped me in my tracks. Curious as to what the little boys were finding so absorbing, I tiptoed over to have a look. If

I supposed them to be immersed in some magical childhood fantasy, building a twig fortress perhaps, or manoeuvring a conquering contingent of pebble soldiers, I was wrong. Two pairs of small hands were meticulously decapitating and disembowelling a spread-eagled and still twitching lizard using an old knife and a pair of nail scissors.

A few weeks later, leaving Lorenzo to supervise the boys' supper, I strolled to the Belvedere for some peace and quiet. It was around seven, the sun had set and dusk was gathering fast. On one side the village loomed above me like a castellated cliff, on the other side the sea rippled silkily out to the lights of fishing boats strung along the horizon. The air was warm, peachy soft and faintly perfumed with garlicky cooking smells. It was a lush, generous beauty and I was filled with gratitude that we had found Torre Saracena and made it part of our lives. I leaned against the parapet, feeling like a bee sucking on nectar.

'*Bella serata, signora, vero?*' a woman commented as she strolled past with a basket of tomatoes balanced on her head.

'*Si, signora,*' I replied. '*Veramente bella.*'

And then, just as I said that, I saw them. A yard or so in front of me, impaled on stakes planted among the huge, leathery cacti and sharp knuckles of rock that plunged steeply from the Belvedere walkway to the beach hundreds of feet below, were three dead cats. Their jaws were open, making it look as if they were screaming silently at the darkening sky. These gruesome totems to an enduring underbelly of medieval brutality brought a chilling sense of menace. It was like discovering a rat in a baby's cradle.

Our own Saracena cat, Micia, was saved by Marcello, Luca and Sandro from a death no less grisly. They presented her to me wrapped in a T-shirt; a trembling, pathetic, newly fledged life entity only the hardest of hearts could have refused. Our no-pet rule was promptly overturned (although if I had known what I was letting myself in for I might have thought twice about giving her a home). It was a dramatic event that became an important part of our family history and, according to the boys, happened like this.

The three of them were returning to the village at the end of a long day on the beach. On the way they stopped at the carob tree where the long black pods that looked like folded bat wings were at their chewable, sugary best. Nearby a group of girls were playing with a skipping rope. Suddenly one of them made the piping announcement that Biagio, the cross-eyed road sweeper's son, had some cats behind the Mill House in Via S. Leone.

Marcello, Luca and Sandro dropped their carob pods and rushed to the scene. Unfortunately, by the time they got there, the worst had been done. In one corner of the scrubby patch was a smouldering bonfire where a mother cat's charred remains belched stinking smoke into the sky. Nearby, Biagio and his whooping friends were taking turns bouncing her still-blind offspring off a high wall. Four kittens had already been killed this way. A fifth awaited the same fate.

The ensuing fight was soon over – mainly because the rescuers were outnumbered and suffered a swift defeat. While his friends pinned Marcello, Luca and Sandro's arms behind their backs, Biagio – a bony 13-year-old in threadbare shorts and a vest – picked up the surviving kitten by its sliver of tail and dangled it in their faces.

'You want it, you pay!' he said, grinning provocatively. 'One thousand lire – not a *centesimo* less.'

One thousand lire, of course, was an impossible sum and everyone present knew it. The price was simply chosen to set the ball rolling for the bargaining that was to follow. These were lean times for the rescuers, however. Birthdays had not come round yet and there was little they could offer. But Biagio would not be convinced. They were foreigners, therefore rich, and they were holding out on him. Picking up a stone he declared that he was fed up with their messing about and was going to smash the kitten's skull. Fortunately at that very moment his brother came running up.

'Dad's got it in for you,' he cried, his pinched face tear-stained and snotty. 'He wants you home.'

The mere mention of the cross-eyed road sweeper was enough to make every boy present shiver. He was a snarling, beetle-browed ogre who fuelled his raging malice with a bitter resentment against life and copious consumption of anisette. Public rows with his short, fierce wife (also an anisette drinker) were a regular occurrence, as was the sight of him battering one or another of his sons with his heavy-duty municipal broom.

Biagio's shoulders instinctively hunched and his brutish swagger left him. He didn't even try to hide his fear.

'OK, you can have the stupid creature,' he muttered. 'Just give me what you've got.'

And so Micia was liberated for the pooled resources of their pockets – 90 lire, a safety pin, and a tangle of elastic bands.

Unbeknown to us, my sister Louise was four months' pregnant when Micia joined our household that summer.

(The village women were more perceptive, however. Pina took one look at Louise the day she arrived and immediately offered congratulations with a knowing smile. And Signora Lucia and Signora Rosalba of the vegetable stall showed her a new respect, calling her 'Signora' instead of 'Signorina'.) So it was with all the warmth of her secretly burgeoning maternity that Louise welcomed the orphaned scrap. She scooped it up, placed it in the big front pocket of her green smock and carried it around like a baby kangaroo, or furry fetus, for the rest of the summer. In due course Micia expressed her approval of this arrangement with a low, rasping purr. Marcello and Luca, who had no previous experience of animals and had never heard the sound before, were terrified.

'We must take her to a vet!' exclaimed Marcello in anguish. 'She's dying of asthma!'

But despite the odd purr Micia showed remarkably little gratitude at being rescued from her fate. She quickly developed a nagging whine and generally behaved in a way indicative of the autocratic, demanding creature she was to become. Within weeks she had us all at her beck and call – all except for Lorenzo that is, who couldn't stand her.

A man with no interest in animals, he complained she looked like a rat and that her presence was further complicating his already difficult life. Nothing would make him happier, he said, than if she decided to disappear and never come back. And the following summer, probably to teach him a lesson, that was almost exactly what she did.

Luca, by now a skinny seven-year-old elf with a toothy grin and debauched-looking shadows under sleepy brown eyes, could beguile even the most crusty and charm-resistant. He was as wily a cadge as any Neapolitan street urchin and most days netted himself an ice cream or two and even a few lire. His look of undernourished waifishness had irresistible appeal. That particular summer, three separate households of foreigners (unbeknownst to each other or me) were feeding him a hearty English-style breakfast each morning.

This charm had not worked with his form teacher in Rome, however. She was deeply disapproving of his long hair and the fact that he had not been baptised. I believed that this was the real reason why she had failed him in Italian, which obliged him to sit a second exam during the summer break or repeat his first year in elementary school. Marcello and I accompanied him back to Rome to encourage him through this unnecessary and unfair ordeal. Lorenzo, who had just started his two-week holiday, was left to look after the cat.

It was a predictably unhappy arrangement. Micia spent their first night sleeping on his chest. Lorenzo tried locking her in the bathroom (she yowled), batting her with a flip-flop (he kept missing) and shouting at her (she turned a deaf ear). Eventually he had to admit defeat. The next morning, bleary-eyed, bad-tempered and determined never to endure such torment again, he shoved her into her travelling basket, took her round to our Argentinian friends and persuaded them to keep her until our return.

The problem was that Micia's near-death experience at the hands of Biagio had left her permanently traumatised and agoraphobic. She would venture as far as our bit of roof or the top of the communal stairs but no further. To find herself in an alien environment surrounded by strangers was extremely disturbing. At first she refused to get out of the basket. And when she did, it was to make a spectacular leap through the window and disappear.

Lorenzo (being only a pretend tyrant) panicked. He knew the distress this occurrence would cause his sons, not to mention, of course, the endless recriminations he would get from me. So for the next couple of hours he scoured the village barking her name and sending every feline in the vicinity scurrying for safety. He then wrote out a reward notice with her description and stuck it on the bar door. For Giovanni this was further proof – not that any was needed – that *forestieri* were quite crazy.

'Two thousand lire for a flea-bitten cat?' he said, cackling with derisive disbelief. 'Shit gold or something, does it?'

The reward notice mobilised hordes of children who arrived throughout the day with writhing, spitting hostages tucked under their arms. It was then that Lorenzo realised his problem: all cats in Torre Saracena are identical. By the evening he found himself with 25 Micia lookalikes ranged around the room staring at him enigmatically. The most unnerving thing, he said later, was the way they all kept so still and quiet – even when he went up to each one in turn and hissed Micia's name in its face. He received the distinct impression that, having assessed the situation as potentially favourable, they were determined not to give away anything that might blow their chances of a comfortable home.

Elimination started by size, then progressed to features Lorenzo was almost certain Micia didn't have (like half a tail, only one eye, or a deformed leg). After that it was down to instinct. Eventually, with just two cats left, he lay on the floor and waited to see which one would attempt to sit on his chest. For a while neither animal moved, then one tentatively approached and sniffed his hair. With that, he decided, the quest was over. The sniffer was given a saucer of milk and the other was booted out. As for the reward, he ended up giving each child who brought a cat a hundred lire.

Having solved the problem, Lorenzo heaved a sigh of relief and went to Stella's for a plate of pasta and *fagioli*. His account of the ordeal was well received and briefly inspired Jasper's plan to turn the Big House into a cat sanctuary.

Returning home at around two in the morning, however, Lorenzo realised all was not resolved. For the moment he opened the door a cat lurking in the shadows outside streaked through his legs, up the stairs, and made a beeline for the fridge in the kitchen alcove. Once there it opened its mouth and began yowling for supper.

The nerve-shredding, haranguing shriek was unmistakable, as was the quivering intensity of the upright tail. The other cat, which had been comfortably curled up on a cushion, now began twitching shiftily and refused to meet Lorenzo's interrogative eye. At this point Lorenzo was obliged to acknowledge that the cat he had recognised as Micia was nothing but a bogus usurper. This was something of a disappointment because in his opinion the impostor was a quieter and therefore much more acceptable animal. Indeed, for a moment he even considered sticking to his earlier choice. But conscience prevailed. The Almost Micia was picked up and unceremoniously evicted into the night.

Marcello and Luca had not the slightest doubt, and never would, that their adored '*Principessa*' was her sublime authentic self and nobody else. Lorenzo also said it had to be her. After all, he reasoned bitterly, could there be another cat so maliciously vengeful as to regularly shit under his – and only his – place at the table?

For myself, the incident left a lingering doubt and there were many occasions during our long and fractious relationship when I found myself wondering. Especially when I would turn to catch her staring mockingly at me through narrowed eyes.

'Silly fools,' she seemed to be saying. 'Conned the lot of you, didn't I?'

Pollo con pepperoni

Every Saturday Signora Lucia returned from the market with a live chicken. She wrung its neck in the bathroom and it graced the family dinner table the following night. Head, neck, feet and giblets were simmered for 3 hours with a bouquet garni to make a fragrant broth. To this she added home-made tortellini and served the soup as a first course. The chicken itself was prepared in various ways. *Pollo con Pepperoni* was one of them.

Feeds 4

1.5 kg (3 lb 5 oz) chicken
50 g (2 oz) prosciutto, cut into strips
2 cloves garlic, crushed flat
1 tbsp fresh marjoram, chopped
½ large glass dry white wine
300 g (11 oz) fresh plum tomatoes, peeled and diced
1 large red and 1 large yellow sweet bell peppers
Extra virgin olive oil
Salt and pepper

Cut the chicken into small pieces. Sauté the prosciutto in a skillet with 2 tablespoons of olive oil; add the chicken and brown all over. Season with salt and pepper, add 1 clove of garlic, the marjoram, and the tomatoes. Continue cooking over a lively heat, moistening with the wine. Cut the peppers into strips and roast them in another skillet with a couple of slugs of olive oil and the remaining garlic. When both chicken and peppers are done, serve the chicken in its juice surrounded by the peppers.

Chapter Nine

THE CHOLERA SCARE

Work started on the port in 1975. The reason was not to provide mooring for the local fishermen (happy to continue beaching their wooden boats on the sand), but to lure the speedboats and yachts of the still elusive Affluent Tourist. In early April a platoon of yellow mechanical diggers moved in to the crook of the rocky promontory that separated our stretch of beach from that of Saracena Mare. Watching them in action was like watching the feeding habits of monster insects. From sunup to sundown the air vibrated with a greedy rasp as great articulated jaws bit ever deeper in the voracious quest for the glossy brochure dream.

Millions of tons of impacted sand were shifted to carve out the basin and concrete was sunk to extend the promontory a further 50 yards into the sea. Part of the plan involved diverting the freshwater stream, obliging women to take their washing to an ugly new fount on the other side of the headland. This was nothing less than a tragedy. The cleft from where the outflow gushed was sealed off and the deep gully of limpid, fizzling cold water was drained and filled in. Never again would women file down the steps to sing and gossip and beat their washing on stones made round and smooth by generations of activity. Never again would dazzling white sheets that were testament to their housewifely skills be spread on the surrounding rocks to dry. One minute the stream was there, the next it was gone. Like a mirage or sleight of hand, it vanished in the blink of an eye and centuries of tradition sank without a trace.

For the foreign contingent the construction of the port cast an ominous shadow. It meant that things were transforming even more radically than we had acknowledged. Unlike the villagers, we had nothing to gain by change and everything to lose. It was inevitable but it filled us with dread. Like obsessive hypochondriacs we saw the most minor modernisations, a new fridge for ice cream at Giovanni's, for example, as symptoms of the fatal disease.

Already there were two new boutiques in the tiny main street and even the haberdashery on the bridge was festooning its doorway with garish beach fashion. Saddest of all was the loss of the Emporio, that magic repository of liquorice sticks and sherbet, crochet needles and great blocks of green and yellow washing soap. On reaching 70, Signora Teresa announced that enough was enough and she was going to retire. She sold the premises to a nephew – a Robert De Niro lookalike lured back from

America by the tourist boom – who spent July and August refurbishing it as a souvenir shop.

All in all, it was a difficult and unsettled summer. The day my friend Hilary arrived from London, Luca was bitten in the face by an unvaccinated Alsatian as big as he was. And as if this wasn't enough, he was further traumatised by an anti-rabies injection administered with a jumbo-sized needle in the centre of his scrawny chest. Barely a week later, Marcello's friend Sandro stayed one night on his way back from Scouts' camp and gave us all worms. Horrified, Hilary and I rushed to the chemist for advice. There we were told that we had been infected by the parasite's eggs getting on linen. Everything, they said, needed sterilising. The mere mention of parasite eggs sent us into shuddering spasms of disgust. For the next two days, sheets, towels and detachable cushion covers (not to mention every item of underwear) were boiled in a battered metal bucket on our two-ring tabletop gas cooker. It was a Herculean task from which we thought we'd never recover.

But it was not only intestinal worms we had to contend with. We had woodworm, too. In fact, the rug chest in the upstairs room was riddled with the creatures. At night the dry grating rasp made by their masticating mandibles rose to a deafening crescendo. And in the morning we always found four or five neat little mounds of sawdust waiting to be swept up. My mother, whose Easter visit the termites had somewhat marred, was very worried. Everything she knew about woodworm told her they would keep on chomping until every stick of furniture, every beam, every piece of supporting timber, crumbled to dust.

To avoid this catastrophe she sent Hilary over with a special poison and the exhortation that we should use it. Every day we would meticulously inject the stuff into each and every hole. My mother had assured us it was absolutely lethal but it wasn't. Or it may have been lethal for English woodworm but their Saracena cousins thrived on it. In the end I was driven to seek the advice of the local carpenter.

As I did not know the Italian word for woodworm, let alone in dialect, he was obliged to come and see for himself. But even at home, and despite my agitated pointing at the sawdust piles, it took a while before he grasped the exact nature of my concern. When he did he was much amused.

'What are you worried about?' he said, grinning toothlessly. 'Torre Saracena is riddled with these *vermetti*, yet it's managed to survive two thousand years. Do you not think it will survive two thousand more?'

One thing that time had not changed was the fact that we were still very poor. That summer the daily budget for Hilary, myself and the boys was the equivalent of £5 in today's money. We did well on it, shovelling away huge quantities of bread, pasta, beans, salad and fruit so that nobody ever went hungry. Our one extravagance was Nutella, which we ate at breakfast spread on thick crusty wedges of freshly baked bread. Other treats were saved to enjoy with Lorenzo at the weekends. One was the welcoming ritual of vanilla ice cream *affogato* (drowned) in gin at Giovanni's. Another was the occasional foray to one or another of the excellent trattorias scattered around the region.

Our favourite place for these culinary feastings was Santa Maria a Morolo, a tiny village an hour's drive into the hilly interior. Straddling a rocky crown above terraced olive groves, it consisted of nothing more than a tight fist of houses clutching a tiny piazza and unadorned church in its palm. The one and only trattoria was run by Alda and Maria, identical twin sisters. It consisted of a single room in which were crammed five or six rough wooden tables, with a couple more on the long, narrow terrace outside. We always made a beeline for the terrace. Roofed with tangled vines and poised like an eagle's nest over the void, it offered a sweeping aerial view over scattered stone cottages and the heaving undulations of the surrounding terrain.

Married to two brothers – and with eleven children between them – Alda and Maria were genius cooks. From their small steamy kitchen came raw marinated anchovies; river snails poached in wine and garlic; ragouts of wild mushrooms; platters of stuffed and roasted aubergines; crispy fried artichokes, and baby onions cooked in vinegar and sugar and eaten cold. There were baskets of focaccia; pies filled with ham, potato and spinach, baked flat and cut into squares; tomato and pepper omelettes; and fat, juicy olives stuffed and fried. The pasta was homemade: *maltagliati* for soups; yellow ribbons of fettuccine, and dumpy little flour-and-water gnocchi served with a simple tomato, garlic and herb sauce. The olive oil in a stoppered glass bottle on the table was thick and green with a strong taste of seasoned wood.

There were six of us the evening we took Hilary there. We arrived around eight and gorged ecstatically for the next five hours. We sampled all the antipasti, then chose the two specials on the menu: peppers stuffed with breadcrumbs, black olives, capers and anchovies,

and an outrageously succulent *melanzane alla parmigiana*.
Between us we polished off a tray of each. After which
a bitter black espresso was all most of us could manage.
Hilary, however, her appetite honed by our habitual
frugality, went on to order a portion of goats' cheese
preserved in oil.

'You'll make yourself ill,' Lorenzo predicted as he
watched her tuck in. And he was right, although
overeating turned out not to be the cause. For, delicious
though it was, that particular batch of cheese turned out
to be contaminated with pathogenic bacteria. Barely
an hour later Hilary was in agony with violent gastro-
intestinal convulsions.

Small communities have a deep-rooted fear of
epidemics and rightly so. Many times during Torre
Saracena's long history, scarlet fever, smallpox, measles,
diphtheria, whooping cough and cholera have swept
through the population with devastating effect. Although
vaccination has brought most of these diseases under
control, cholera is still a peril. In the south particularly,
contaminated seafood is a common cause. Only a
couple of years earlier, in fact, mussels infected by the
raw sewage pumped into the bay sparked off a major
outbreak in Naples. Among the deaths was a relative of
Peppino's, which, for the Saracenesi, brought the tragedy
even closer to home.

The epidemic was certainly on the doctor's mind
when I knocked on his door at 3 a.m. He listened,
stricken with horror, to my lurid description of Hilary's
symptoms and it was only with the deepest reluctance
that he agreed to come and take a look at her. And
'look' was the operative word. For when we arrived he
refused to risk anything more than a quick peek into

the bathroom where Hilary was crawling on hands and knees between the toilet and sink.

'This is a disaster,' he moaned into the large handkerchief clamped to his face. 'I'm calling an ambulance. That woman must be got out of here!'

Forty minutes later the ambulance was in the Piazza. The noise of its engine at that untimely hour brought many anxious people to their windows. What they saw was Hilary's limp body being hoisted into the back of the vehicle by myself and the ambulance driver. Keeping a safe distance, and still with the handkerchief over his mouth, was the doctor. Within minutes of our departure the agitated medic was surrounded by a small crowd demanding to know what was going on. Which was how the whole cholera scare started.

Our destination was the largest hospital in the region. Throughout the journey, in the pauses between one intestinal seizure and another, Hilary ventured fearful questions about the standard of hospitals in southern Italy. Given the situation I thought it better to lie. What reassurance I managed to give, however, was destroyed the instant we arrived. For lined up on the front steps of the dilapidated and peeling edifice we found a committee of hysterical medical staff waiting to bar our entry. In one voice they shrieked, 'She can't come here! We haven't got the facilities! Take her to the Spilanzani in Rome!'

We arrived at the Spilanzani, the hospital for tropical and contagious diseases, around 10 a.m. Hilary was tucked into a narrow iron bed with inset potty, the sole occupant of a dingy, cavernous room situated down the far end of an echoing, marble-floored corridor. In fact, she appeared to be the sole occupant of the entire dusty wing.

'It's been so nice and peaceful here recently,' whispered the old nun, leading me away from Hilary's prone body. 'We must pray to the Blessed Virgin that your friend isn't the start of anything nasty.'

With Hilary safely deposited, I made my way back to reception. It was there that the reality of my own predicament hit me. Firstly, I had not brought my bag which meant I was stranded in an unfamiliar part of the city without money, identity card or keys to my flat. Secondly, under the flimsy bit of market tat that passed for a dress, I was stark naked. If it had not been for the absence of underclothing, however, I doubt the nuns would have been helpful. As it was they had mistaken my dress for a nightgown, which further worked in my favour.

'Well, it's obvious the Signora can't wander the streets in her nightgown without knickers,' ruled the brisk nun in charge. And she promptly picked up the phone and arranged for the same ambulance that we had come in to drive me back to Torre Saracena.

The vehicle had to be disinfected before leaving. It drove around the rambling hospital complex to a special shed where I got out and two men sprayed the inside with several litres of pungent liquid. When I was allowed back in, the broiling midday sun beating on the roof had transformed the interior atmosphere into that of a steamy tropical greenhouse. Choking on the fumes, I stretched out on the bed and, dizzy with exhaustion, folded my hands across my chest and immediately fell into a deep sleep.

I slept dreamlessly until the driver stopped at a bar in Saracena Mare. While he was gone, faces pressed curiously against the ambulance window and shrill voices debated whether or not I was dead. 'Yes she is,' one opined. 'Look at her waxy sheen.' They got the fright of their lives when I suddenly opened my eyes and sat bolt upright.

Meanwhile the old town was in the grip of collective hysteria. At 7 a.m. – and witnessed by a large audience – a squad of men carrying huge metal canisters and wearing what looked like white spacesuits arrived to fumigate our flat. Lorenzo was fast asleep when they burst into the bedroom like storm troopers. He and the boys were given five minutes to wash, dress and get out. In no time a rumour was circulating that we indulged in shameless 'mussel orgies', and that mountains of mussel shells were regularly seen piling up outside our door. Suddenly we became not only foreign, but also untouchables. Even Signora Lucia's front door stayed firmly closed. Marcello was refused entry to the Piccolo Bar in the New Piazza, Luca was spat upon and both were called *'colerosi'* (cholera carriers). As for garlic – nature's own intestinal antibiotic – people were ingesting it by the kilo and by evening Torre Saracena's entire stock had sold out.

This state of frenzied alarm persisted for 24 hours. During this time the entire outsider community came to be suspected of consuming contaminated molluscs, prompting Lorenzo to march a group of the children to the doctor for anti-cholera shots. At the height of it all, Stella fell down the trattoria stairs and broke her arm. Jasper managed to borrow a car and she was seen being driven out of the village white-faced and groaning with pain. Both Brunetto il Piccolo and Billy tried to defuse the tension by testifying as to what had happened, but nobody believed them. They were convinced she was

Victim Number Two of the cholera plague about to be unleashed on their heads.

In the end, all that was needed to restore calm was Hilary's timely return the following day, well rested and glowing with health. For her the whole experience had turned out very nicely. Not only had her 'cholera' been nothing more than food poisoning, but she had also found romance in the person of a young doctor with an Emiliano Zapata moustache. (They made their entrance roaring into the Piazza on his Ferrari-red Moto Guzzi motorbike.) Stella's reappearance with her right arm encased in plaster from wrist to armpit also helped, although her mood was considerably less radiant. For one thing she had spent 16 hours waiting to be X-rayed (because of an impromptu strike). For another, her inability to brush her bristling bush of frizzy hair had transformed it into a snake pit of medusan knots. Once back, and without a word to Jasper, she went to the barber's and had the whole lot shorn off.

With the all clear sounded, Signora Lucia returned to her doorstep. As atonement for her lack of solidarity (which I completely understood), she gave me a bottle of the rather acidic white wine produced by a brother-in-law. Neither of us were feeling particularly cheerful so we passed a satisfying half-hour indulging our pessimism. We complained about everything: husbands, children, rising prices, the new port, loss of hallowed traditions. Even the cholera scare was mentioned – but only in the non-personal context of the government's poor record of protecting public health.

'Well,' she said with a sigh, when the approach of suppertime brought our lament to a close. 'They say that every cloud's got a silver lining. If such a thing can be believed, of course!'

As it turned out, however, the cholera scare did have a silver lining of sorts. Apart from Hilary's romance, which kept her happy for the rest of the summer, the problem of the woodworm was solved. Suddenly the *chomp chomp* noise ceased and there were no more piles of sawdust waiting to be swept up in the morning. Our first thought was that the larvae were tired and were giving their jaws a rest. Then it dawned on us that they had actually been exterminated by the spacesuit-clad fumigators sent by the council. My mother was delighted.

Cipolline in agrodolce

The food poisoning incident did not deter us from returning to Alda and Maria's *trattoria* two weeks later – although we steered clear of goat's cheese! It was the usual feast and it lasted hours. One of the antipasti was *cipolline in agrodolce*, or sweet and sour baby onions. I served them quite often myself, usually to accompany a simple meal of bread and cheese.

Feeds 4

800 g (1 lb 12 oz) white baby onions
3 tbsp white wine vinegar
½ tbsp sugar
2–3 slugs extra virgin olive oil

Peel, wash and dry onions. Sauté them in a wide pan with the olive oil until golden. Turn down heat and simmer with the lid on until onions are tender. Mix the sugar with the vinegar and add to the pan. Cook briskly for a couple more minutes or until liquid is rich and syrupy. Serve cold.

Chapter Ten

LEONE AND HIS
BROTHERS

Beach life was a culture of its own, with its own manners, dress and social pursuits. For the hard core of Torre Saracena habitués it was a *salotto*, an extension of the ritual gathering at the bar each morning. At Giovanni's the tribe drank bitter black coffee, blistered their tongues on the napalm-hot jam at the heart of Salvatore's freshly baked *cornetti*, read *L'Unita*, *Manifesto*, *Il Male* and other left-wing publications, and voiced loud, provocative opinions on the country and state of the world. (The bar, of course, is the Armchair Revolutionary's natural habitat. And although none of us wished to define ourselves as such – with the exception of a German couple on the run from a Baader-Meinhof past – Armchair Revolutionaries were all we were.)

Political debate and gossip continued down at Leone's where our untidy occupation turned patched and faded umbrellas into miniature gypsy encampments. Clothes hung like gaudy streamers from every sagging spoke, tattered beach towels carpeted the sand, food, babies, pet dogs and bottles of mineral water were stashed in the cool shade. Naked children ran amok, adolescents postured and flirted and there was constant toing and froing between umbrellas to play cards, chess, read someone else's book/magazine/newspaper and, of course, talk.

Talk among women generally fell into four categories: children, sexual politics, sex itself and cellulite. This last – an Italian concern decades before the British discovered it – was bemoaned, railed against and every aspect of its dimpled detail endlessly discussed. Modesty was non-existent and it was common to see exasperated sufferers, alone and in groups, vigorously manipulating the despised excess on their buttocks, bellies or rippled thighs. Less public was the 'hydro-massage' championed by some as the most effective way of banishing the curse. Followers of this method spent tedious hours wading up and down bum-high in the sea. A more diverting variation was the 'hydro-twist'. This involved energetically swivelling legs and hips to create a powerful swirl that slapped fat around like loose bags on a pole.

Another beach issue was suntans. The Torre Saracena hardcore cultivated a laid-back approach (three months guaranteed a good tan, anyway). Unless forced by very young children to descend early, it was not cool to appear on the beach before midday or early afternoon. Those on shorter holidays felt differently, of course. For them a tan was a high priority and they approached the act of sunbathing with a nuptial anticipation of fulfilment and bliss. (As did my mother, whose skin was paler than most – so pale, in fact, that seen from a distance she dazzled like bones bleaching in the sun.)

The amount of effort used to achieve the desired hue was a source of idle amusement to the rest of us. The careful oiling, meticulous adjusting of swimsuit and towel followed by the ecstatic surrender of splayed limbs to the sun. And ten minutes or so later the whole reverent ritual would be repeated. Nobody talked about skin cancer then and warnings of the dangers of overexposure were rarely heeded. As Kristina, a regular visitor from the Swedish island of Gotland, said: 'How can I worry about flaking skin? The sun is my awakener. I am a flower hungry to bloom after a long Arctic night.' Her attitude changed, however, when she got severe sunstroke and collapsed over a bowl of Leone's mother's mussel soup.

The reason for frequenting Leone's rather than Tullio's was that Leone was young, welcoming and for several years gave credit to even the most unprepossessing of us. As with Tullio's, the original wood hut kitchen and adjacent bamboo-roofed eating area had expanded with each passing year. By 1976 there was an ice cream and soft drinks' kiosk, and a long veranda with tables and a jukebox. Tucked away at the back were two much-appreciated flushing toilets.

Leone was the eldest of nine siblings, the others being Fiorella, Leonardo, Pietro, Giovanni, Matteo, Marco, Gino and Patrizia. They were tall, well built and for the most part handsome. This was especially true of Leonardo who looked like a film star, with a perfect nose, sulky lips and a crown of burnished, copper-coloured curls.

By contrast, their father was small, bent, toothless and prematurely aged – as, indeed, was his wife. At first sight it seemed a genetic miracle they had managed to produce such well-favoured offspring. In fact, their physical aspect was simply a mirror of the poverty and struggle that had been theirs until summer visitors arrived to change their fortunes. Even with money flowing in, however – more of it every year – they found it hard to alter their ways. The mother railed against the extravagance of changing her wood-burning stove for a modern gas cooker. And the father continued rising at dawn to put in long hours on his three acres of land.

This heartless and stony patch was situated between the beach and the coast road. To irrigate it, water was pumped by hand from deep wells and distributed by a system of hosepipes that ran alongside the narrow paths and bamboo windbreaks that criss-crossed the terrain. The main crop was tomatoes, but spinach, onions, garlic, lettuce, courgettes and broccoli were grown too. There was also a small olive grove, lemon and apricot trees, a few goats and a dozen or so scrawny hens. Growing in wild abundance everywhere were great spiny clumps of prickly pear. It was Leone's father's proud boast that until the youngest, Patrizia, was born, the family had never eaten anything he had not caught, grown or bartered for.

During the summer season the only one who could be spared to help him was Pietro. Marco and Matteo waited tables, Giovanni ran the kiosk, Leonardo was in charge of the umbrellas and Fiorella worked in the kitchen with her mother. Leone was the man who kept it all together, the one who dealt with complaints, solved problems and generally coordinated it all. Gino, Marcello's age and an aspiring drummer, was allowed to spend much of the day bashing away on his petrol can drum kit in the middle of a tomato patch. But he also had his chores, as did Patrizia.

Fiorella, the second eldest, was tall like her brothers with a long face accentuated by the headscarf she tied, peasant-fashion, over her hair. Whereas they were handsome and vigorous, she was plain, heavy-limbed and moved as though burdened with overwhelming lethargy. Of all her family she was the most fascinated by the *forestieri*. In the summer of 1971, aged 23, this fascination blossomed into a full-blown crush (long-distance and undeclared) for a young American hippy in our group. In fact, Paul – or Poll as she pronounced his name – was her main motive for cultivating a friendship with me. She wanted to know how old he was, what sort of girls he liked, why he often looked sad, and any other snippet I could think of to tell her.

When she was not talking about Paul, Fiorella wanted to know how much money Lorenzo earned, whether I had a washing machine, and what sort of lives people led in London and Rome. Her own life, she complained, was dismally boring. Unlike the boys she was given no pocket money, had no opportunity to make friends, and if she went anywhere – even to the village – one of her brothers had to accompany her. Her father was very strict in that respect and even her mother never went anywhere alone. Her one dream, she said, was to marry a rich man and live in a big town. Any big town, it didn't matter. Just so long as she could spend every day going round the shops.

The following year she became friendly with a family from Turin. She would chat with the wife, play with the children and always give them special attention on the occasions she waited at their table. Before they left they presented her with a ceramic brooch and asked if she would like to take the place of their mother's help who would soon be leaving. Not only would she receive the princely sum of 10,000 lire a week, but she would also have her own room with TV and en suite bathroom.

Fiorella's determination to accept this wonderful opportunity caused a family crisis of mega proportions. There were daily rows with her mother – frequently during the lunchtime rush – and screaming confrontations with her brothers. On his return from work the father sat in his chair on the veranda, silent, unapproachable and unmovably grim. The dark shadow cast by this bleak monument to parental outrage had a cowing effect on all of the sons. Only little Patrizia was unconcerned.

'You know what?' she said to me blithely one day. 'Papa says that if Fiorella goes to Turin he'll never take her back. Not even if she comes crawling to him on hands and knees.'

Fiorella, however, was clearly undeterred by this threat because she left before the summer was out and stayed away for five years. Having witnessed the more public aspects of the drama we tactfully avoided asking for news or even mentioning her name. As far as we were concerned it was out of sight, out of mind and after a while most of us forgot she had ever existed. Then in 1976 she suddenly reappeared. She was much thinner, bony almost, and her hair was dyed red and cropped as short as a boy's. The real surprise, however, was not so much her appearance. It was the moon-faced toddler with chocolate-brown eyes who clung to her thighs and called her mama.

The official word was that the child was the fruit of Fiorella's failed marriage to a no-good Torinese. But the real truth – eloquently expressed by the bitter and unforgiving back now turned on her – was that little Andrea was a bastard whose existence trumpeted the shame and dishonour now staining the family name. For this Fiorella was treated as a pariah by all of them. She was ignored, given no work (Pietro's wife and sister-in-law had replaced her in the kitchen), and she was even obliged to take her meals alone. She seemed to accept this savage ostracism stoically. She spent her days reading romantic fiction, chain-smoking contraband Marlboros and making listless sandcastles for her little son. Several of us tried to be friendly, to show that we were on her side, but she did not want to know. A tangible aura of hurt and distrust surrounded her like a wall.

The person who made the most effort was Cora. As an unwed mother-to-be she considered herself Fiorella's natural ally, which was why she was so persistent. In reality, they had nothing in common. Cora, a sexy starlet from Holland, had been impregnated by a well-known married film director of bedroom comedies. Not only was she unfazed by the scandal their liaison had caused, she welcomed it. For she was the first to recognise that attention from the paparazzi had done more for her professional visibility than any of her acting roles. This attitude was reflected in her defiant refusal to shroud her pregnant belly in maternity beachwear. Instead she let it balloon triumphantly between bikini bra and bottom like a golden-brown seedpod straining to burst.

It did not take long for the paparazzi to track Cora to Torre Saracena. And when they did they used a telescopic lens to snap her canoodling with her squat, balding lover on Leone's veranda. The resulting pictures, typically fuzzy, were published in the largest circulating gossip magazine under the title: 'While Cora and Fabrizio Await The Birth of Their Love Child, The Betrayed Mother of His Five Children Weeps Alone.' The main picture showed Fabrizio leaning across the table to give Cora a lingering kiss. In the background, clearly recognisable as they stared at the couple with pointed interest, were Leone and his father.

Within hours of the magazine's arrival at the newsagents, all the village knew of Cora and Fabrizio's wickedness. But even infamous celebrity has a powerful magic and for a while the Saracenesi were sufficiently dazzled to suspend their disapproval. More dazzled than anyone were Leone and his family. Not only was their veranda and section of beach featured in a national magazine, but the head of the family and his eldest son had also been anointed with instant fame. A framed copy of the spread – screaming title and all – was given a proud place above the till on the kiosk wall. Cora was deferentially fêted and fussed over while Fiorella looked on bleakly. The irony was cruel.

Cora left to prepare for her Big Event just before the storms that mark the passage from August to September. These meteorological extravaganzas are invariably preceded by several days of mounting electromagnetic tension. During this time the air compacts, heat densifies and tempers detonate along a fractious edge. Hot gusty winds whip up high, foam-crested waves enticing children and able-bodied adults alike to bodysurf until salt water streams from every gasping orifice and brains throb in dizzy rhythm with the crashing breakers.

The storms themselves are of primordial ferocity. The huge basin of glowering sky echoes to the deafening boom and crack of thunder. Wild forks of jagged lightning slash through the shuddering stratosphere to unite heaven and earth. The surface of the sea turns a heaving, churning, seething black. Below the surface a frenzied push and pull of lashing currents rework the gently rippled bed into a perilous landscape of steep cliffs and swirling vortexes. Violent squalls give birth to funnel-shaped waterspouts which spin across the mist-shrouded horizon like ghostly imprints of a whirling dervish's ecstatic dance. And when the rain finally comes it falls in blind, heavy sheets that turn the sand into gullied mudbanks and make fast-flowing rivers of the village streets.

Like most people, I usually made sure I was home before the deluge occurred. That summer, however, intoxicated by the wild tumultuousness of it all, I lingered too long and was caught on the beach. Leone had sensibly closed shop and I ended up sheltering under a jutting ledge of corrugated roofing at the back of the kitchen. Pressed up against the wall, listening awestruck to the magnificent roar, it sounded as though the universe had sprung a gigantic leak.

Ten minutes or so passed, then somebody appeared round the corner and dived for shelter beside me. It was Fiorella. She was soaked to the skin and the hair plastered around her face looked like a fluted red bathing cap.

'*Ciao*,' she said, and proffered a wet and crumpled packet of Marlboros retrieved from the waistband of her shorts. 'Want one?'

We smoked in silence while the deluge continued to rage around us. When it was over we walked to the top of the wooden steps leading from the veranda to the beach.

'What happened to that *americano* friend of yours?' she asked suddenly. I looked blank. 'You know, the nice-looking one who was always clowning around and had blond hair down to his shoulders.'

'Paul?'

'*Si, si*,' she said. 'That was his name. Poll!'

It was only halfway through telling her he had died of a heroin overdose that I remembered her big crush on him. But Fiorella didn't seem upset. She just nodded expressionlessly and lit a fresh cigarette from the stub of the old.

'I had a friend in Florence who died of a heroin overdose,' she said. 'He shot up before going to bed and when I woke in the morning I found him dead beside me. Still, who's to say he isn't better off? After all, life's shit – no?'

While I was trying to think of something to say, a child started to cry. It was a thin, insistent wail originating from the family's sleeping quarters out in the back. As she monitored the sound Fiorella's expression softened, then she smiled contentedly.

'Andrea's teething, otherwise he's as good as gold,' she explained, flicking her smouldering cigarette butt into the air. It traced a brief, glowing arc before plummeting to earth. 'We'll be moving to Rome this winter,' she continued. 'If I can get a job, that is. But even if we stay here a while longer, it doesn't really matter. I'm never bored now, you see. That baby's far and away the best thing that's ever happened to me.' Then she turned and walked quickly away.

The sound of the child had lassoed her heart and was reining her in.

Gelato all' uva

September is the month of the grape, when towns and villages all over Italy hold *la sagra dell' uva* to celebrate harvesting the fruit for wine making. For the village, which had no wine festival, the advent of the August/September storms meant grapes would soon take over the market. Like most people all I wanted to do with sun-ripened grapes was wash and eat them (and in copious quantities too!). Tammy's mother, Jane, however, was inspired to make this fancy sweet with grape ice cream.

Feeds 4

1 litre white or red grape juice
4 egg yolks, lightly beaten
250 ml double cream
Icing sugar
Little bunches of grapes, washed and dried

Dip the grape clusters into the grape juice to moisten, then into the icing sugar to coat. Place the grape clusters on a small tray and freeze until frozen, about 4 hours.

Put the grape juice into a saucepan, bring to the boil and reduce by half. Remove from heat and add egg yolks, stirring constantly. Add cream, strain the mixture through a fine sieve and put the saucepan back on the heat, then cook gently until the mixture thickens slightly. Remove from the heat and leave to cool. Freeze until required.

Serve the ice cream garnished with the sugared grapes.

Chapter Eleven

FESTA DEL PAESE

The panoramic coast road linking Torre Saracena to the national network of highways was built in 1954. Until then, perched in rocky isolation, the town existed in a medieval time warp ignored by, and separate from, the rest of the world. In those days the village economy was dependent on fishing, olives and, later, tomatoes. People rose to their labour before dawn and bedded down at nightfall. Many families lived in one room with a cooking stove on one side, and an ancient bedstead big enough to accommodate six on the other. In the space between – beneath low beams hung with bunches of herbs, rounds of smoked goats' cheese and stiff boards of dry salted fish – there was a scrubbed wooden table and hardbacked chairs. The only decorations were pictures of saints and the Virgin Mary.

Signora Lucia spent her early childhood in just such a dwelling. Such was the deprivation that she still remembered her mother's pleasure on finding a sheet of newspaper someone had dropped in the street. Once home she would fold it in half, cut the bottom into a pretty scalloped edge and use it to decorate a shelf. She shared the huge family bed with her parents, two younger sisters and paternal grandmother (a second mattress was unrolled nightly for the other siblings who slept on the floor). They continued this arrangement even when the grandmother lay dying.

'We just squashed up to give her more room,' Signora Lucia explained. 'And anyway, she wasn't aware of anything. She looked at us but she didn't see us, she saw the faces of her dear departed. Her soul was already winging its way to the other side. The night before she died she was talking to her husband, dead himself fifteen years. "I'm fed up with all this," she told him. "I'm coming to join you." And when we woke the next morning she'd gone.'

According to Billy, things were much the same in the fifties. Despite television, greenhouse tomatoes and the few outsiders who had bought property, poverty and overcrowding were still the rule. The sufferings of birth and death could be happening in the same room and intimate experience of both was inescapable. Billy himself, during the year he lived with his lover's family, shared a room with his lover, a brother and an old uncle who fell ill and died after an agony lasting a week. To escape the sound of the old man's death rattle, Billy spent the nights wrapped in a blanket on the Belvedere. It was winter, the season when Torre Saracena hunches bony shoulders and withdraws deep into itself. When Billy recalled that lonely vigil he shivered. He remembered waiting for a life to end with only rats, foraging cats and the unsolved mysteries of the universe for company.

Providing much-needed respite were the village festivals. These eagerly anticipated events were the historic high spots of the communal calendar or, as someone grandiloquently put it, the glittering thread running through the harsh weft of daily reality. There was pomp and ceremony, music, dancing, games and toothsome things to eat. Children ran wild, lovers found occasion to flirt, and a pungent smell of mothballs trailed families done up in their Sunday best. The village put on its most shimmering face (decorations for the festivals being a matter of great civic pride). Illuminated arches of filigree delicacy were erected along the promenade in Saracena Mare and at the two entrances to the old village itself. Long ribbons streamed from street lamps and multicoloured fairy lights were strung all around the Piazza, across the bridge and from balconies everywhere.

The itinerant traders (who serviced all the village festivals of the region) arrived around mid-morning to start setting up their stalls. They sold cheap plastic toys, trinket jewellery, sugar-coated nuts, candyfloss, nut chocolate and great chewy slabs of pink and white nougat. At Easter there were also stalls selling newly hatched chicks whose downy fluff had been dyed every colour of the rainbow. Crammed together into big cardboard boxes, these sad, shivering little creatures barely survived long enough for the children who bought them to get them home.

Of Christmas and Easter, the Easter *festa* was the most important and each year a sizeable number of Torre Saracena's emigrant sons returned from around the world to celebrate it. On Good Friday a torchlit procession bearing a statue of Jesus Dead and the Madonna in Mourning wound its slow, hymn-singing way from Saracena Mare up through the old town to the tolling church. A second procession on Easter Monday carried the Resurrected Jesus and a Resplendent Madonna to the walled cemetery half a mile away. Villagers sheltered from the sun in the shade of tall, sombre cypresses while the fat, sweating priest celebrated mass.

The Festa del Paese took place in August. It was a bit like the village's birthday, as it celebrated San Rocco and San Leone – Torre Saracena's official patron saints – and was therefore both a religious and civic affair. (All Italian towns have an official patron saint – or three – as does every profession from dentist to prostitute.) The procession was headed by an altar boy carrying a crucifix, followed by children dressed in white for their first communion. Next came the priest under a white and gold silk tasselled gonfalon. He was followed by the mayor, alderman and local chief of police. Next in line was the hunchback, Gino, bearing the municipal coat of arms. Behind him came eight men carrying the brightly painted and lavishly robed statues of the two saints. After the saints came the brass band, and finally the cortège of villagers brought up the rear.

The procession ended at the candlelit church. During a solemn ceremony the priest sprinkled the statues with holy water and blessed them. After this he gave the signal for the congregation to come forward one by one and pin offerings of money onto the saints' dresses. It was a ritual in which the Christian virtues of meekness and humility played no part. The notes were stapled together in a wide, ostentatious fan to ensure the exact generosity of each contribution was clearly visible to all.

Although one Festa del Paese tends to be indistinguishable from another, that of 1977 was memorable for two reasons. Firstly, the village awoke to discover the beach littered with what appeared to be thousands of red and white crabs, but which in fact turned out to be packets of Marlboro cigarettes. (The story was that they had been washed up during the night when a smugglers' boat dumped its cargo overboard while being chased by the *Guardia di Finanza*, the Excise Office.) Nobody could believe their eyes. A Dionysian god had showered the village with manna from nicotine heaven. There was a mad stampede as people crammed pockets, plastic bags, cardboard boxes, and any other container to hand with the miraculous bounty. On closer inspection, however, it was found that the cigarettes were sodden with salt water. Even after being dried out the taste was so foul it made them unsmokable. Nevertheless, the village was left in a state of thrilled disbelief. The whole thing felt like a grand-scale magic trick expressly performed to get the *festa* off to a kick-start.

Reason two was that the Saracena Vecchia band was finally selected over the rival Saracena Mare band to provide the musical entertainment in the Piazza. Not only was it a success that had eluded them for five years, it was also the occasion Leone's brother, Gino, made his drumming debut.

One of the reasons it had taken so long was that the Saracena Vecchia band had a history of mishap and discord. There was a bass player who fell off a roof and broke both wrists, a singer who left after dreaming of the Virgin Mary telling him to become a priest (he took a job on a cruise ship instead), and finally a dispute between two members over a deal involving fake Cartier watches.

This last was a particularly bitter affair and almost caused the band to break up.

That year, however, they had a new singer, a new bass player and a new drummer. Wearing smart suits, bow ties, and with neatly brushed hair they trooped onto the stage looking like throwbacks to the well-scrubbed fifties. Their repertoire consisted of mainstream favourites like *'Volare'* and *'Blu Blu L'amore é Blu'* interspersed with Italian versions of past and present Eurovision Song Contest hits. During the course of the evening each of the instrumentalists was given a solo spot to demonstrate his virtuosity. When Gino's turn came he was spectacular. Arms wheeling, legs kicking, head swivelling, practically levitating with inspired frenzy he was, as Jasper said admiringly, 'the demon drummer from Hell'.

The crowd packing the Piazza and the tables outside Giovanni's bar applauded enthusiastically. The outsider kids, sprawled on the steps and balustrade of the Big House, gave him a howling, stamping, whistling ovation. 'Bravo, Gino!' they bawled, punching the air. *'Sei forte!'*

Because he lived on the beach, Gino was also an outsider of sorts. He had crossed barriers and made real friends among them. Furthermore, they had followed and encouraged his progress on the petrol can drum kit from the very start. He was one of them and in his moment of triumph they were justly proud.

Also proud were his family. Dressed in their formal best they occupied the central position immediately in front of the stage which was patriotically festooned with red, green and white rosettes and Italian flags. During Gino's impassioned solo Leone took pictures while the father and mother unfurled enormous white handkerchiefs to wipe away tears. Fiorella was also there with little Andrea who was trussed into a suit and bow tie like those worn by the band. Standing next to her was an older man I had never seen before. He had a kindly face and picked Andrea up to comfort him when he started to cry. (She later confided that he was a cousin from Montreal and had offered to take her and the boy back to live with him at the end of the summer.)

The performance concluded shortly before midnight with a thumping rendition of 'Crocodile Rock' chorused in made-up English because none of them had managed to learn the words.

Then it was time for the climax of the celebrations: the fireworks display. As with the illuminations, the quality of the fireworks was a matter of civic pride and every village strove to make theirs the most spectacular. Italian taste, particularly in the south, demands that fireworks are heard every bit as much as they are seen. This means that even the most modest starburst detonates at such a booming, ear-splitting volume that everything in the vicinity vibrates. Made in Naples (home of pyrotechnic wizards) in lean-to factories that regularly blow up, these combustible artistries have never come cheap. Nevertheless, even the smallest and poorest of hamlets will find the funds to put on a light-show extravaganza.

The fireworks were set off on the road that ran beneath the promontory connecting the old town with the new. The main reason for this location was to ensure the display was visible to (and therefore admired by) neighbouring towns and villages along the coast. For the staid or elderly the best vantage point was the Belvedere. For the young and agile it was the craggy descent that flanked the stairs leading down to the new port.

Being young and agile, Gino and his fellow band members made for the latter. Drunk with success, they joked and laughed their way over to a space by the rusted iron cross erected centuries back to ward off evil blowing in from the sea. Unfortunately their high spirits were soon to be dampened. For sitting on the rocks immediately below were the two sisters of the drummer of the other band.

The girls, both in their teens, were very pretty and very hostile. They lost no time in voicing their opinion of the Saracena Vecchia band which, in a nutshell, was a 'pathetic joke'. As for Gino, their brother's particular rival, well, he was the 'most pathetic joke of all'. In fact, his 'demented display' meant he was now the laughing stock of the entire village. Furthermore, the only reason they'd been selected over the far superior Saracena Mare band was because the entertainment committee had been bribed. Because the girls were so attractive the counterattack was slow in getting off the ground. Once it did, however, there was no holding back and they exchanged insults until the fireworks started and drowned everything else out.

The main hazard of the displays was fall-out. Every now and then flaming debris spiralled out of the sky to nose-dive into dry clumps of vegetation and set them alight. On this occasion – possibly karmic retribution for her previous vitriol – the first target of the night was not vegetation but one of the sisters. Spinning giddily from the tail of an exploding rocket, an incandescent fragment settled like a firefly on her thick mane of waist-length hair. Her response, and that of her sister, was to fling herself about in flailing panic. While this was going on, Gino leaped forward and deftly plucked it out. Like a rogue Tinkerbell it then danced onto his lap and, before he could brush it off, burned a smoking hole in his smart new trousers.

Back in the village the stalls were being dismantled, as was the merry-go-round known as *calcio in culo* (meaning 'kick up the arse'), with wooden seats hanging on chains from a central pole. It was called this because the object of the ride was to grab a ribbon dangling off to the side, an achievement only possible with a kick from the person behind. The gambling wheel, however, tucked away behind the fountain near the bridge, was still going strong. There, a small huddle of old men, frisky with aperitifs and wine, were betting on a spin of the hand-painted wooden wheel. Among those enjoying a flutter – technically illegal but nobody bothered – were the ex-mayor, Giovanni, Signora Lucia's husband, Gaetano, and Berto the Fascist with his polished shoes, Toscano cigar and foppishly long, thickly-oiled, dyed black hair.

Also present, though not betting, was a man known as Marcia Imperiale. Once the elementary school teacher, his mind had been tipped into madness by the deprivation and suffering he endured during the Second World War. Since then he had spent each day delivering speeches exalting Italy's past glories to invisible audiences. It was these orations, liberally peppered with fiery slogans from the old regime, that gave him his name (*Marcia Imperiale* being a reference to Mussolini's conquest of Ethiopia). His other passion was composing verse tributes to Torre Saracena which he transcribed on notebook-sized bits of paper and posted on walls around the village. He lived in constant terror of another war and always carried a plastic bag containing items necessary for survival in the hills.

That night, as well as the plastic bag, he also had an accordion strung around his neck. After a lengthy and passionate address that began, as many of them did, '*O glorioso Romano Impero*...!' he heeded the demands to shut up and started to play. Fortunately, madness had in no way affected his musicianship. His fingers skipped deftly over the keys and immediately the notes of a lively tarantella rose to fill the balmy night air. Suddenly it was a *festa* from another age. The old men smiled happily and began rhythmically shuffling their feet.

'*A Giovà*,' Berto the Fascist called to Giovanni in dialect. 'Remember how we used to prance around?'

Giovanni cackled. 'That was over fifty years ago, but I remember. You were the best partner I ever had!'

'Come on, then,' said Berto. 'Let's give it another whirl now.'

Clasping each other firmly round the waist, they went up and down, round and round; a little stiff and arthritic maybe, but still managing to keep up the fast, skipping step. Others soon followed, including the ex-mayor and a thin old man who barely came up to his chest. A small crowd gathered to watch and clap their hands in time to the beat. Some of the older women were moist-eyed, including Benedetta's mother who was there with her butcher son.

'You know, Signora, this reminds me of when I was young,' she said nostalgically. 'In those days all the bachelors danced together unless, of course, they were formally engaged. For myself, the first time I danced with my husband was on my wedding day.'

The next morning it was all over. The illuminations were taken down and all that was left of the decorations were torn fragments of paper streamers caught on bushes or trampled into cracks. The Marlboro packets had been cleared from the beach and it was business as usual at Leone's. Gino was helping one of his brothers in the kiosk. His euphoria had evaporated to be replaced by gloom – partly due to anticlimax and partly to his mother's fury over the ruined suit. Then in the afternoon the sisters of the rival drummer turned up. They bought two ice lollies and the one with the long hair gave him a keyring with a little furry teddy attached.

'What's this for?' Gino demanded, still angry and resentful.

'To thank you for last night, of course,' the girl replied with a demure smile.

Gino struggled to resist her seductive appeal but lost. 'Last night?' he capitulated with a reluctant grin. 'So what happened last night, then?'

Noci zuccherate

Of all the goodies on sale at the festa sugared nuts were a top favourite. Tammy – she of the Swiss flag and glowering rages – was particularly partial. As part of the constant effort to keep her daughter sweet, Jane devised her own version.

460 g (1 lb 1 oz) brown sugar
230 g (8 oz) white sugar
Large carton sour cream
300 g (11 oz) pecan nuts
300 g (11 oz) almonds

Combine the sugars and sour cream in a large saucepan. Cook over a medium heat, stirring until the sugar has melted. Continue cooking but stop stirring (the mixture will become granulated again if you go on). It is ready when a little mixture dropped into cold water makes a small ball. Remove from the heat. Add the nuts and stir gently to ensure they are thoroughly coated. Place them on a marble or non-stick sheet – separating nuts that have stuck together with a fork – and leave them to dry and go crispy.

Chapter Twelve

STELLA'S ROMANCE

By 1978 Stella had been living in Torre Saracena for nine years. The village had long ceased to hold any enchantment for her and the only reason she stayed was because the trattoria – not withstanding its ever falling culinary and hygienic standards – still provided an income of sorts. Despite this grudging attitude, however, the years had turned her into a curious foreign/native hybrid. She was fluent in the dialect (although she scorned speaking it), her daughter had gone through the local school, and the shapeless, dark-patterned dresses she favoured were indistinguishable from those worn by the Saracenesi women. Of the small clutch of resident outsiders she was the only one to undergo such a metamorphosis. One reason for this was that, as a trader earning her bread by tourism, she was a contributor to the local economy and shared its concerns. (The others, being freelance creatives, derived their income from the wider world.)

But there was something else, too. On some strange level, Stella seemed to understand the village's darker psyche. And that darker psyche understood her.

Jasper, on the other hand, was still exactly the same. The only difference was that he now spent large chunks of the year in Rome and Berlin. Occasionally this was due to film work (the offers he received came almost exclusively from German underground cinema), but mostly it was just to hang out. Hanging out was the art form closest to Jasper's heart, his only real vocation. He particularly liked hanging out in cafés and bars, being either brilliantly entertaining or a crashing bore. The main thing he was dedicated to, however, was doing whatever he wanted with supreme disregard for anyone else. So when in Torre Saracena, he partied and openly philandered. Eight years younger than Stella, he was a narcissist and a ruthless Pan. His quarry were the nubile, overexcited arrivals ensnared by the predatory pulling power of his supple body and sexy mane of sun-streaked hair. He set them up and waited for them to fall. And fall they did, dropping their knickers with such speed you were almost deafened by the twang of snapping elastic.

Most of them soon regretted it, however. For behind Jasper's rut-and-strut lurked a fear and dislike of women. One thing guaranteed to bring this to the fore was seeing a girl in control and feeling good about herself, at which point he would embark with sadistic relish on a campaign to cut her down. Humiliation and abasement were central to all his dealings with the female sex. Over the years he had honed his spite into an instrument of the most precise torture.

On one occasion he stage-managed the simultaneous humiliation of both Stella and Mary, Tammy's 18-year-old Irish au pair, with whom he was having an affair. During the siesta hush of an August afternoon he took his freckle-faced inamorata to the room above that where Stella sat crocheting. Knowing the acoustics were such that Stella would hear everything, he first made loud love to Mary, then subjected her to an outpouring of contemptuous abuse. Then he went to the bar, leaving her in hysterical tears.

Stella neither confronted Jasper with his maltreatment, nor confided in anyone. Her response was to retreat ever further behind biting sarcasm and aloof disdain. She was a combination of psychological bully and emotional coward: a porcupine with poisoned quills. And although she tolerated the other women rather than blaming Jasper himself, they still got lashed by her pitiless tongue. But despite everything, her ferocious efforts to maintain dignity often moved me. Watching her closed face and up-thrust chin, the ramrod stateliness of her careful step as she crossed the Piazza, I could see the wounded life she nursed within.

She was almost 50 now but looked much older. Her slimness had long since turned scraggy, revealing a landscape of stringy tendons and sharp joints beneath her lined and lacklustre skin. A sad loss was the glorious halo of outrageous frizzed hair. Since cropping it in the summer of the cholera scare, she had never grown it again. Cutting her locks seemed to drain the last of her erotic energy. She was emotionally and physically juiceless. Her sap had dried up. Like the middle-aged women of Torre Saracena, Stella had donned the black shroud of sexlessness.

Regardless of whether they liked her or not, most outsider women were angry and exasperated at the humiliation Stella put up with. Of the original bunch, at least a third now had different partners to those they were with when they first arrived. Divorce was now legal in Italy and even mainstream couples were separating for much less than Stella endured. In this context Stella's behaviour was not merely incomprehensible but insulting to women generally. Tammy's mother, Jane – who had left her sculptor husband, Nato, for a Chinese painter – likened her to a battered wife who was too emotionally damaged either to leave her abuser or press charges. Others maliciously said that at her age Stella probably felt that even a lousy man was better than no man at all.

The women of Torre Saracena saw it differently. The new divorce laws meant nothing to them; indeed the first village annulment wasn't until 1985. A husband was a husband and, good or bad, that was that. For many unhappy women, widowhood was still the only release they could hope for. Very occasionally, however, circumstances offered another way out. An example was Maria Pia, one of three sisters who ran Bar Sole, the winter bar, on the bridge. Her husband's pathological jealousy was rivalled only by that of old Giovanni. Despite being a devout woman leading an impeccable life, he accused her of conducting a secret liaison with every man who glanced in her direction. He also objected to her going to weekly confession, arguing that if she had done no wrong she would have nothing to confess.

Although obedient to him in everything else, Maria Pia refused to compromise her religious faith. So the husband then confronted the priest and demanded to know what his wife's secret sins were. 'Nothing that concerns you, my son,' the priest replied, turning his back in pious dismissal. These words confirmed all the man's worst suspicions. He punched the priest in the face, then ran home and stabbed Maria Pia with the knife she was using to gut fish for lunch. As she sank to the floor in a pool of blood the police burst in. Happily, the blade missed anything vital and she survived. Her husband, on the other hand, was sentenced to twenty years for attempted murder.

It was Stella herself who told me the story. Over the years she had become friendly with the sisters whose dour and reserved ways were sympathetic with her own. During the winter when Jasper was away and the trattoria closed she was a regular visitor to their chilly, austere bar. With customers few and far between, the four of them spent many an afternoon sitting around a Calor gas stove drinking lemon tea, eating sugared biscuits and crocheting. Jasper called the sisters 'The Three Witches' because he suspected them of saying unflattering things about him behind his back. He also refused to set foot in their establishment unless someone else was paying. Over the business of Stella's romance, however, they were the first people he went to begging for advice.

Stella's romance started in September, less than a week after Jasper left for yet another trip to Berlin. It was a fairytale courtship, not least because it had seemed impossible that such a thing would ever happen to her again. Only the day before in fact, a split in the wooden seat of a rickety chair had pinched her bottom. Her sour comment was, 'I suppose I should be grateful for the gesture.' Furthermore, the fact that her suitor hailed from Berlin – the very place Jasper was once again deserting her for – seemed justice of the most divine kind.

Everybody noticed Dieter when he walked into the Piazza. He was tall, pale, with small round glasses and an uncanny resemblance to John Lennon – which explained the screeching children who trailed him from the bus in the excited conviction he was the real thing. He was also wearing a long, flapping black raincoat which, considering the temperature, was eccentric indeed. He was accompanied by the French jazz clarinettist Pierre D., his host and a long-standing Torre Saracena regular. They stopped briefly at Giovanni's for a *caffe corretto* – coffee with grappa – after which nobody saw him again until that evening when they both turned up at Stella's.

The trattoria in 1978 was not the place it had been. Over the years a steady drain of energy and optimism had resulted in overcooked pasta, flabby lasagne, sticky risotto and inedible seafood salads. Certainly the peaks achieved during the summer of Mob's glorious culinary exploits had never been rivalled. Stella made no secret of the fact that she hated both cooking and most of the people who came to be fed (and all of Signora Assunta's various successors apparently felt the same). That evening the main item on the menu was a soup concocted of fish scraps that had been languishing in the fridge. The result was an unappetising, unfragrant, greyish slosh that made my stomach give a bilious heave when I lifted the pot lid.

Despite this, it had all gone by the end of the evening. Not only that, but Dieter claimed he fell in love with Stella at first sight – which was of her coming towards him swathed in a grubby white apron bearing a bowl of the stinking broth.

'What's in it?' he asked, smiling into her sour, set face.

'Piranha fish,' she replied coldly.

'What else?'

Dieter was 29 and an art historian. Moreover, he was good-looking and solvent and there were several attractive and available young women more than eager for his attentions. But Dieter had eyes for no one but Stella. That first inauspicious exchange had touched his heart and his single-minded courtship began then. Forsaking the pleasures of the beach, he trailed Stella around the morning market ready to lug the heaviest of the bags back to the trattoria for her. Within days he had established himself as her right-hand man, her supporter, her adoring swain. But it was no S and M, slave/mistress game that he was playing. He wanted her for his woman. And at every opportunity, and regardless of who else was present, he told her so.

At first Stella treated Dieter with the same caustic disdain she treated everybody else. He was not deterred. On the contrary, it seemed to make him even more determined. But in truth, Stella was a fortress long ready for storming. It took only a few days of this passionate assault for her defences to come crashing down. The trigger was provided by the underage daughter of a Roman psychiatrist and his doctor wife.

A precocious flirt, the girl had made a beeline for Dieter the moment she spotted him entering the trattoria. Within minutes she was all over him, stroking his hair, blowing in his ear, and attempting to twine her arms around his neck. Whereas Jasper would have been delighted at these attentions, Dieter was not. He grew increasingly irritated and eventually told her to 'piss off'. These words sprung the catch of Stella's closed heart. When the kitchen closed she joined Dieter at his table and they polished off a bottle of the trattoria's best white wine together. That night Dieter shared Stella's (and Jasper's) bed. And there he stayed until the time came for him to leave.

Stella's softening was in just the right measure. She retained the sharp wit that defined her, but lost the spite. And she smiled a lot more, which really suited her. Not that we saw much of her. The lovers spent most of the day either cloistered in Stella's flat or going for long drives in the jazz musician's red Ford convertible. And if anything she cared even less about the trattoria than she had before. On more than one occasion she simply did not bother to open at all.

Ten days or so into the affair they took off for a honeymoon week at a twelfth-century monastery, now a hotel, clinging to cliffs above Amalfi. Claudia, thirteen and typically difficult, stayed with me. Ellen, a wild child from Boston with a manic style of eloquence, was left in charge of the trattoria. Many of the main dishes she produced were inedible – especially the pasta – but she made up for that with her cakes. Every night there were flaky apple pies, meringues filled with whipped cream, brownies, banana cake, nutty ginger biscuits and a variation of a chocolate Swiss roll.

Word of the affair eventually reached Jasper roistering in Berlin. He responded by going on a two-day drinking binge – during which he got into a brawl and was almost arrested – then catching the first available flight back to Italy. He missed his rival by a hair's breadth, for Dieter had left just the night before. By then the lovers knew they were destined for each other. The pain of their parting was lessened by knowing that, after sorting things out in Torre Saracena, Stella and Claudia would be joining Dieter in Berlin.

When she told Jasper he was devastated. Pride in pocket, he went around begging anyone and everyone to tell him what had gone on in his absence. He wept, beat his breast and hung his head in guilty shame when told he deserved everything he was getting and more. His distress was real, of that there was no doubt.

'If she leaves me I'll die,' he declared. 'She's the only woman I have ever loved. I'll do anything to win her back.'

Jasper was given lots of advice, mostly to do with treating Stella with respect and paying her proper attention. He didn't actually need any of it, however, because he proved he could be as inspired a wooer as anyone when he wanted. Early every morning he rose from the sleeping bag to which he had been banished and set off into the hills in search of wild flowers. He would return an hour or so later with his arms full and proceed to rouse his slumbering lady by scattering fragile scented blossoms over her bed. (Stella said it wasn't the caress of petals that woke her but the horrible creepy-crawlies that came with them.) On a more prosaic level he re-whitewashed the trattoria, replaced Dieter on the morning market round and stopped chasing other women. All in all he became everything a model mate is supposed to be.

Meanwhile Dieter was making daily phone calls from Berlin. He missed Stella, longed for her, and was ready to send plane tickets for her and Claudia the moment she gave the word. She was not to worry about her financial security, he said, because she would earn much more giving private English lessons than she did slaving over a stove. But if teaching did not appeal, that was not a problem either. His university salary would support the three of them in reasonable comfort until she found something she did want to do.

But despite all the reassurance and love, Stella dithered. Suddenly the whole thing looked like a big, risky leap in the dark. Lack of money and the fact she did not speak German were certainly influencing factors. The other was a new anxiety that Jasper planted in her mind about the 20-year age gap. What about when Dieter was 40 and she was 60? He might promise the earth now but did she really believe he'd still be around in ten years' time?

So in the end Stella stayed, which was a disappointment to those of us who had encouraged her to be brave and follow her heart. 'Age is only a problem if you make it one,' we insisted. 'Older women and younger men are part of the European culture – just think of Colette and her young lovers.' Another argument was, 'Better a year in a wonderful relationship than a lifetime with someone who grinds you under.' And more bluntly, 'If you let this chance go you might never have another.' We also warned her that Jasper would lose no time in reverting to his old ways once his position was re-established and things were back to normal.

Which was exactly what happened. No sooner was Jasper back in Stella's bed than he abandoned it for Ellen's from Boston. It was an affair designed exclusively for punishment and revenge, conducted to inflict maximum hurt and humiliation. To this end he made a public display of their sexual liaison: touching, bickering, strolling the village hand in hand. And to add insult to injury, when the trattoria opened for the off-season weekend trade, Jasper insisted his mistress be wined and dined for free. They also took to breakfasting at the winter bar on the bridge. Jasper did this not for the coffee, but to savour the ferocity of Maria Pia's hate-black eyes.

Stella was not the same woman she had been before Dieter, however. She still avoided direct confrontation but there was a tangible difference in the steely aloofness she once again assumed. Gone was the sense of shored up misery. Instead we were aware of a tense resilience underpinned by new resolve. And then, in the first week of December, Ellen returned to the States. Jasper hung on for a few restless days before deciding it was Berlin-time for him again. He sailed out on the one o'clock bus wearing the brown and yellow chequered donkey jacket Ellen had bought for him at the Saturday morning flea market. Saverio, waiting for a daughter to arrive from Matia, was the only person around to wave him goodbye.

Billy invited Stella and Claudia to share his Christmas turkey. Later in the afternoon other friends crowded into the small flat for wine and sweet refreshments, including his ex-lover and family, and Maria Pia with her two little nieces. There was chatter, music and a roaring log fire in the stone hearth. Billy, more than a little drunk, was reminiscing about the brave and spirited woman Stella had been in the days when they had known each other in Florence.

'Torre Saracena's not good for everyone,' he said sadly. 'It's been good for me, but it's not good for you. Not anymore.'

'So?' Stella replied dryly. 'What's new?'

Billy bought Stella out of the trattoria. He also helped her find a small apartment within walking distance of the Pantheon in Rome. Shortly after moving in she bumped into an old friend who gave her a job writing English subtitles for Italian films. She also went into partnership with Maria Pia selling their hand-crocheted cot blankets and baby clothes to an expensive children's boutique.

Jasper – who this time had no tip-off – breezed back a couple of months later to find nothing of his life left standing. Stella and Claudia were gone. Billy was planning to relaunch the trattoria as a bar-cum-jazz club called The Blue Angel. The Big House, once again shuttered, was now destined for conversion into five self-catering holiday flatlets. The lock had been changed and it took him three days to retrieve his possessions, stuffed by Stella into rubbish bags and dumped in the hall.

Convinced that Stella had gone to live with Dieter after all, Jasper was once again plunged into despair. He spent his days with the old men in the back room of Giovanni's hunched tearfully over his beer. Elio, still his number one fan, was shocked to see his hero so pitifully diminished.

'A man must never put himself at women's mercy,' he said sternly. 'They're not worth it. Around here we say the longer the hair, the shorter the mind!'

Arturo, a grizzled octogenarian who had spent forty years working in a car factory in Detroit, turned from his card game to nod in agreement.

'Yeah, they stab you in the back as soon as look at you,' he growled. 'Better a snake than a woman. Take it from me.'

Pasta e fagioli

Stella was that rare creature: an Italian who professed no interest in food. Her own diet consisted principally of rusks dunked in black tea. This explained why she was such a careless and indifferent cook. Of her more palatable offerings, *pasta e fagioli* – pasta and bean soup – was Lorenzo's favourite. Not only can one find versions of this peasant dish all over Italy, but housewives individualise it, too. This recipe is my own version.

Serves 4

200 g (7 oz) pancetta/guanciale affumicata
(alternatively thick-cut smoked streaky bacon); the
fattier the meat, the better the flavour
3 x 450 g tins of good quality Italian borlotti beans
(when buying, shake tin; if beans knock against side
that's good, as it means they're not mushy)
300 g (11 oz) small pasta tubes called 'tubetti'
(alternatively other chunky soup-type pasta)
Stick of celery, chopped
Bunch parsley, chopped
3 cloves garlic, chopped
1 medium onion, chopped
300 g (11 oz) fresh plum tomatoes, skinned, de-seeded
and chopped
Extra virgin olive oil
Salt and pepper
Optional – chicken stock cube
Toasted bread to serve

Sauté onion, garlic, celery and parsley until soft. Dice the guanciale/pancetta affumicata or smoked streaky into cubes and fry until lightly golden. Add the tomatoes, season with salt and pepper. Cook on a slow heat until liquid thickens (think tomato sauce). Add beans together with their liquid and optional chicken stock cube. Now add the pasta. If there's not enough liquid, top up with boiling water during cooking. When the pasta is roughly twice its original size (pasta in soups does not have to be as al dente as in the dry dishes), adjust seasoning and ladle into warm bowls. Serve with toasted bread rubbed with garlic and more olive oil.

Chapter Thirteen

MAKING MONEY

Stella's romance was one thing talked about that year. Another was Lorenzo stepping in to save a six foot seven mentally handicapped teenager from a thug. It happened on a Saturday in August, at an hour when summer people lazed on the beach and village women prepared lunch. Among the handful of stragglers still slouched over coffee and newspapers at Giovanni's was Lorenzo. He was joined by Luca who was on a mission to replace a pair of flippers he'd lost. Given his record for losing things – anything not an organic part of him eventually went missing – Luca decided that to get cash out of his father he would have to be smart. So instead of asking for a handout he tried pitching for a loan. Lorenzo gave him a brief, impatient hearing. At the point where Luca started explaining that repayment would be made when someone bought his Roman treasure (a thin spiral of tough blue glass found in the rubble of a nearby archaeological site), he cut him short with his trademark growl. Then he returned his attention to the political scandal reported in that morning's *Paese Sera*. And there it stayed until a dark blue Alpha Romeo came roaring over the bridge and into the Piazza.

This macho violation of the sultry, indolent calm caused papers to lower and conversation to stop. Giovanni's stragglers watched with narrowed eyes as the vehicle rocked to a halt outside Peppino's bar and a thickset man carrying a briefcase got out. Alerted by the noise, Peppino himself appeared. Visibly agitated, he ejected his single client (the cross-eyed alcoholic street sweeper) before ushering the man inside and quickly closing the heavy door. The stragglers exchanged meaningful glances. What they were witnessing seemed to confirm that a rumour currently doing the rounds was true. The rumour was that Peppino, who everyone knew was mixed up with contraband trafficking, had fallen foul of his criminal associates in the nearby port town. These guys had beaten him up and were now squeezing him for money too.

Minutes passed. The driver, thickset like his companion and wearing a Fruit of the Loom T-shirt, grew hotter, sweatier and increasingly bored. Then Bartolomeo rounded the corner and he perked up. Here was an opportunity for some welcome *divertimento*. With an ugly leer he followed the lad's slow shuffle towards the narrow alley which took him home. Bartolomeo's shorts hung like bags and his enormous, ulcerated feet were wrapped in dirty bandages that trailed loose ends through his sandals. Restarting the engine, the driver slipped the handbrake and nudged the car forward until the bonnet was touching Bartolomeo's thigh. Then he began hooting and nudging, hooting and nudging, sniggering with amusement as a terrified Bartolomeo staggered and thrashed in an effort to keep his balance.

Lorenzo, a man who rarely exerted himself physically and certainly never hurried, moved like greased lightning. One minute he was sitting at the table, the next he was standing by the Alpha Romeo smashing his fist on the roof.

'*Figlio di puttana!*' he bellowed, eyes bulging and veins the size of hosepipes throbbing in his neck. '*Pezzo di merda!* What the fuck d'you think you're doing?'

At this the driver sprang from his seat like a crazed jack-in-the-box. '*Froscio! Coglione!*' he screamed back. 'Who do you think you are touching my fucking car? Do it again and you're dead!'

Instead of replying, Lorenzo turned to the traumatised youth and began calming him down. He was joined by our Argentinian friend Raul, who took Bartolomeo's arm and began leading him away. Meanwhile the driver continued with the spit-flecked cursing. Then, without warning, he reached under the T-shirt and pulled a Beretta from the waistband of his jeans. This did not have the intimidating effect he expected, however. On the contrary, it unleashed the full force of Lorenzo's disgust and contempt.

'Look at this prick!' he cried, with reckless disregard for his own safety. 'He's not just an ugly little bully. He's a complete cretin, too!'

Luca, watching the drama from the sidelines, was torn between pride and panic. To him it was like a live-action replay of the key scene in *High Noon* (a tattered copy of which still got an occasional screening at the open-air cinema), with Lorenzo in Gary Cooper's starring role. Even the lighting was the same: the arching sun carving the semi-deserted Piazza into zones of dazzling brightness and inky shadow. And then the gun was produced. Despite having grown out of his religious phase, Luca begged God to intervene before bullets started flying and his father bit the dust. And God, it seemed, was listening. For at that precise moment Peppino's door reopened and the man with the briefcase came striding out.

'*Andiamo!*' he snapped, getting back into the car. '*Presto!*'

With seething reluctance the desperado stashed away his firepower. Then he hunched his shoulders toughly and swung his bulk back behind the wheel. His parting shot to Lorenzo was, 'Your days are numbered, *stronzo*! I'm going to get you!'

Lorenzo shrugged off these words but Luca didn't. The driver's description was circulated to a network of children who kept a lookout for the rest of the summer. At first there were false sightings every day, which wasn't surprising given that short stocky men populated the region. One poor innocent, wearing a clinching Fruit of the Loom T-shirt, was stalked by a gang of glowering ragamuffins for a whole day. And not at a distance, either – whenever he turned around they were breathing down his neck. Desperate to escape them, he scuttled down to the beach and paddled his lilo out to sea. For a cunning while they let him think he'd succeeded. And then suddenly they were there, swimming in menacing circles around him. Eventually things calmed down. Furthermore, abject grovelling got Peppino readmitted to the criminal fraternity (or so it was said), so there were no more roaring Alpha Romeos around. And in the unlikely event that the driver did come back, he did so quietly and wasn't recognised at all.

Lorenzo's impetuous action fitted his image. Despite a sober job in marine reinsurance he was a Che Guevara lookalike with politics to match. (It was his radical views and air of dashing wildness that I initially fell for. And these same things kept me enamoured, offsetting the constraints of his job which paid little and, for much of the time, obliged us to live a far more conventional life than I would have chosen.) He inherited his politics from Orazio, his resistance-fighter-turned-Communist-senator father; the unkempt appearance was his own.

Orazio was immaculately groomed and something of a dandy. He disapproved of Lorenzo's scruffiness and particularly the long hair. Indeed, he even resorted to giving Lorenzo 'barber money' so he could make himself 'decent'. When it came to his grandsons' shaggy locks, however, Orazio had no complaint. In fact, he was charmed. This was mildly disappointing to Marcello and Luca as they would have liked barber money too. Instead their handouts came from a game invented by Orazio to mock his own vanity called 'How Do You Find Me?' On arriving for a visit he would fling open his arms and demand, '*Allora*? How do you find me?' To which the boys' chorused reply was, '*Bellissimo, nonno! Bellissimo!*' for which they were each rewarded with a coin. He continued to repeat the question, soliciting ever more complimentary answers, until his pockets had been emptied of loose change.

Being children of cash-strapped parents, loose change was something Luca and Marcello were always on the lookout for. Marcello and his friend Sandro, like many of their peers, had no qualms about begging. '*Ciai na piotta*?' ('Got a hundred lire?') was the standard request to adults who looked as though they were liberal or left-wing. Luca, on the other hand, was more industrious. At the age of five he was offering translation services to lost-looking tourists who wandered into the Piazza. He introduced them to Brunetto il Piccolo and took them to Benedetta's *alimentari*, which now stocked Kellogg's cornflakes, Nutella and even chocolate Nesquick. He also told them bloodthirsty stories about villagers frying invading pirates in cauldrons of boiling oil. When it came to payment it was 'stuff' not money he was after: ice lollies, *gassosa* (lemonade) and jam doughnuts.

As he grew older that changed. Hard cash replaced 'stuff' as his prime motivator. He became an eager errand-runner, prepared to shop or retrieve items people had forgotten at home for as little as 50 lire. Then at the age of eight, Stella (a shameless exploiter of underage labour) gave him his first proper job. It entailed sweeping floors, setting tables and shelling the prawns that were slopped up from the port in battered plastic buckets. Luca was OK with sweeping and setting, but the shelling he hated. Apart from the fact that he was deeply repulsed by the beady-eyed, feeler-waving crustaceans' resemblance to giant insects, an hour spent pulling their heads and shells off left his fingers stiff and sore. The day he was instructed to help Natalia clean cuttlefish, however, showed him that some jobs could be even worse.

Natalia was a skinny 13-year-old remarkable for having one blue eye and one brown. She hung around the trattoria not to earn pocket money, her hairdresser parents gave her plenty, but because she enjoyed it. This was fine by Stella. Natalia cooked at home and had skills the trattoria found useful – preparing shellfish being one.

As the elder and more experienced child, Natalia got to wield the knife. After removing the heads, cuttlebones, guts and ink sacs, she passed what was left to Luca for rinsing under the tap. It was a messy business, particularly when the ink sacs burst and they both got splattered. What made the whole business gruesome, however, was that she accompanied removing innards and gouging out eyeballs with stomach-churning conversation. She started with an account of her cannibal goldfish eating its tank mate (it bit chunks of living flesh out of its side). This was followed by a roadkill story (flattened squirrels spilling their brains), a description of her aunt's deformity (born without thumbs), eventually arriving at haemorrhoids.

'It was the worst thing ever,' she gloated, describing a photograph she had seen in a medical textbook. 'There was this fat man bending over with a bunch of purple grapes hanging out of his bum. Or that's what I thought they were until I read the caption!'

That did it. Sick to the stomach Luca tore off his apron and left. On the way home he bumped into Claudia and Tammy. Not only did they sympathise with his ordeal, but Claudia declared that working for her mother was the absolute pits. She then confided that she and Tammy were about to embark on a new venture: making jewellery out of pasta and selling it. Luca was impressed. In fact, his reaction was so enthusiastic the girls decided he should be allowed to join them.

The next morning, following step-by-step instructions in the 'Fun Things To Do' section of one of Claudia's comics, they set to in our kitchen and produced the first batch. This involved tipping different shapes and sizes of small, truncated tubes of pasta straight from the packet into a dry frying pan and toasting them. After five minutes of vigorous shaking, the uniform whitish colour gave way to a stunning mix of straw-yellows, caramel-browns and almost-blacks. After which they threaded the cooled pieces on to fishing line (donated by Tammy's mother, Jane) and tied a knot at each end to stop them falling off. The artistry lay in the creative combining of shapes and shades, which they did very well. In fact, most of the necklaces, bracelets and anklets were extremely pleasing.

Initially they flogged their creations to parents and friends of parents. Then some older children took a fancy to them and suddenly festooning oneself with *tubi* and *tubetti* was cool. At the height of this brief craze they had a pitch beneath the carob tree on the steps leading to the beach. They worked it with the persistence of North African street urchins, pestering and wheedling everyone who passed. They even did so in foreign tongues. '*Kaufen! Kaufen! Sehr gut preis,*' for example, and '*Regardez joli collier. Très bon marché!*' Americans were their favourite customers, oohing and aahing and never questioning prices that doubled at their approach. They also tended to be philosophical when the stuff fell apart a day or two later.

The problem with pan-toasted pasta jewellery as made by Luca, Tammy and Claudia was its brittleness. People went out wearing a pretty necklace and returned dangling a near-empty piece of fishing line. Not surprisingly, this had a negative effect on product desirability and once the novelty wore off business dried up. This was a big disappointment to the entrepreneurial trio who had become used to affluence. With no customers and no rewards the hours spent camped on the steps became mind-numbingly boring – so much so they got into the habit of distractedly crunching on their unsold wares. At first it was just the odd nibble here and there. Then one day their spirits sank so low they abandoned restraint and ate the entire stock. It was the day they ceased trading.

That year Luca's plan was to make money from fishing with his friend, Carlo. The idea came after Carlo's 18-year-old uncle lent them a speargun and they managed to harpoon a large fish. They took it to Tullio who, after identifying it as an *orata*, bought it for 1,500 lire. At that moment their aquatic playground acquired a new dimension. It was now a repository of riches as well as a place for surfing and fun. The *orata* was caught at the port so they concentrated their efforts there. For a whole week they went every day, encountering nothing but jellyfish and tiny fish that swirled around in glittering shoals. The community of old fishermen who spent their days smoking and confabbing on the stone jetty advised them to try their luck elsewhere. 'Fish don't like it here, it's too busy,' they said. 'Go to Punta Mare. You might even find sea bass there.'

Punta Mare is a steep cliff of jutting rock with a ruined thirteenth-century lookout tower perched on the top. It takes ten minutes to get there by boat. As Luca and Carlo did not have one, they were looking at a good half-hour swim. Despite enjoying an enviable freedom within the boundaries of the village, children were strictly forbidden to stray further, and where the sea was concerned, the slightest risk-taking sent me into a panicked frenzy. Consequently, the expedition was organised with the greatest secrecy.

On the appointed day Luca, Carlo and three friends struck out from the outcrop of rocks at the far end of the beach. Although they felt like a crack platoon, their equipment was pathetic. Between them they had one mask, one speargun and – because Luca had failed to obtain money to replace his pair – a single flipper.

The sea was calm, the swim a doddle. On reaching Punta Mare, Carlo (as provider of the all-important gun) dived first. After shooting and missing a couple of 'whoppers' he handed the mask, flipper and speargun to Luca. Luca had his go, then handed over to the next boy, and so on. When Luca's turn came round again instinct told him he was going to be lucky.

The cliff fell in a sheer drop before vanishing into darkness. This time, instead of diving wide of it as he had before, he hugged closer. He'd only gone a short distance when he saw two round eyes above a chilling array of snaggleteeth staring at him from a crevice. It was a moray eel, a snake-like monster capable of severing a boy's head from his body with a single bite! Seconds later he was breaking the surface gasping in terror. He managed to get a grip on himself and, encouraged by his friends, returned to try and bag it.

It was on his way down that he spotted the octopus, dramatically magnified by the mask, drifting gracefully several feet below him. The adrenalin rush was like a kick from a mule. He took aim, fired – and missed by a whisker. The enraged octopus convulsed violently, turned a deep purplish-red and attacked, wrapping its tentacles tightly around his left ankle. Fortunately for Luca, eight pairs of eyes had been dipping in and out of the water to monitor his progress. The moment he started struggling, his pals came diving to the rescue.

Rescued with him was the octopus. Its grip was so tenacious that Luca had no alternative but to swim back trawling it behind him. The group's arrival was witnessed by a man collecting sea urchins (local wisdom said the roe, eaten marinated with oil, garlic and lemon, was a powerful aphrodisiac). Chuckling with amusement he prised the three-kilo Jules Verne monster off Luca's ankle, then flipped its head inside out and beat it for a good five minutes on a slab of rock. As someone who objected to people squashing spiders or killing flies, Luca found this extremely disturbing (although spearing fish hadn't bothered him at all). Even the creased 5,000 lire note Tullio paid for it could not justify the cruelty. It was only later, when the five of them sat down to a feast of ice cream, Coke and wedges of Salvatore's succulent pizza, that he was able to put it out of his mind.

The following day *risotto con polipo* (octopus risotto) made its appearance on Tullio's menu. I know this because Orazio, who paid us a surprise visit, took us there for lunch. Normally Luca would have been thrilled by the treat. But on this occasion, fearful of his unauthorised adventure coming to light, we had to drag him along. Despite the fact that Tullio himself was absent – apparently in Naples to buy a spare part for his car – Luca could not relax. And he refused the *risotto con polipo* (understandably) choosing instead *spaghetti al pomodoro* which he scoffed in two minutes flat. After which, announcing he was suffering from sunstroke and needed to lie down, he sprang from the table and bolted. With no temperature and the appetite of a horse this was obviously a lie. Nevertheless something was wrong and my maternal intuition soon supplied the answer. Luca, I decided, was suffering a delayed reaction to the confrontation between Lorenzo and Bartolomeo's tormentor.

'Imagine how powerless he must have felt!' I said as my eyes filled with tears. 'I mean, his father was in mortal danger. The effect on such a sensitive child would be devastating.'

Marcello, who knew all about the octopus business, sensed an emotional drama brewing. 'Don't worry about Luca,' he said gruffly, hoping to avert it. 'He's not sensitive. He's just a *testa di cazzo*, that's all.'

This comment did not go down well with Orazio. Although he tolerated things in his grandsons that he condemned in his son – long hair for example – bad language was not one. Calling his brother a 'dickhead' got Marcello sharply rebuked. Luca, on the other hand, profited from the misinterpretation of his malaise. I cuddled him, Lorenzo promised a game of chess and Orazio sacrificed his post-prandial siesta to take him for a walk.

On their return Luca was quite restored. Orazio claimed that a man-to-man exchange about 'feeling powerless' and 'dealing with fear' had done the trick. On hearing this Marcello, forbidden from uttering another profanity, snorted. He knew what had restored Luca's grin and it wasn't the talk. It was the new pair of cellophane-wrapped flippers tucked securely under his brother's skinny arm.

Risotto con polipo

Tullio's thin, downtrodden wife learned to cook at her grandmother's knee and never weighed or measured anything. Tammy's mother, Jane, did. This octopus risotto recipe is hers.

Feeds 4

1 kg (2 lb 3 oz) tenderised octopus, cleaned and prepared
400 g (14 oz) Arborio rice
6 tbsp olive oil
Large glass red wine
3 large onions, chopped small
2–3 cloves garlic
1 sage leaf
Handful minced parsley
Salt and pepper

Bring to the boil a large saucepan of water to which has been added 1 chopped onion, 1 large glass of red wine, salt and pepper. Add the octopus, reduce the heat and simmer for 1 hour (don't overcook or it will go rubbery). Remove when tender, conserving the broth. Chop the octopus into inch-long pieces. In another saucepan sauté the remaining onions, the garlic, sage leaf and minced parsley. Add the rice and broth, calculating 2 cups of broth to 1 of rice. If necessary add more broth during the cooking. When the rice is ready stir in the chopped octopus and serve.

Chapter Fourteen

THE TOPLESS RIOT

M y mother is an English lady in every way. Her relationship with the village was based on mutual courtesy and respect. She is also a woman of many talents, of which languages is not one. Almost from the day of my marriage she made diligent efforts to learn Italian. With the exception of '*si*' and '*no*', however, and the phrase '*sono una studentessa d'italiano*', she had not only failed to retain a single word, but was unable to distinguish it from Spanish and Portuguese. Despite this, she managed extremely well. When buying meat, for example, she first mimed the animal and then slapped haunch, shoulder, belly or chest to indicate the cut. For chicken she flapped her elbows and squawked, for lamb she baaed, for pig she discreetly grunted.

She was particularly popular with Signora Rosalba of the vegetable stall. Their special relationship started the day my mother attempted to buy the eggs she knew Signora Rosalba sold but were not that day on display. What she intended to say was '*Sei uova*' ('six eggs'). What came out, however – memorised after long consultation with her pocket dictionary – was '*Sei uomo*' ('you are a man'). Signora Rosalba politely denied this, my mother insisted and the resulting conversation grew progressively bizarre. Fortunately Louise's now four-year-old daughter, Bella, possessed a large vocabulary of Italian words. On noticing her grandmother's difficulty she left her playmates and came to the rescue with the correct word. The misunderstanding caused much delighted laughter. Signora Rosalba sent her son back to the repository to get the eggs. Bella was scooped up for hugs and kisses and my mother left with an extra '*uomo*' donated free.

My mother was also on excellent terms with Signora Lucia and her husband, Gaetano, with whom she communicated via smiles, gestures and a glowing good will. Everything about her won their approval: her beauty, elegance and, more than anything, the prodigious amount of time she spent shopping and cooking. For when it came to providing nourishing English meals for her three grandchildren, my mother made no concessions to either culture or climate. Mozzarella was fine, as indeed were salads, but they did not make for a *proper* meal at the end of a long and energetic day.

So every day, with temperatures in the searing nineties and valiantly ignoring the sweat streaming from every pore, she produced cauldrons of chicken soup, huge, hearty stews, great piles of sizzling chips, platters of fried sardines and – much despised by the children – mountains of healthy boiled greens. Sadly, the lack of an oven prevented her from making the wonderful cakes and biscuits we so appreciated. She did manage steamed suet puddings, however, which she served piping hot and drenched with honey.

Her eccentric insistence on this ill-suited cuisine amused everybody. Nevertheless, the succulence of the steamy aromas wafting down to the Piazza regularly enticed people into making 'impromptu' visits around suppertime (served at English time at least two hours before anyone else). One of these visitors was Tammy's mother, Jane, who experienced her first-ever bubble-and-squeak at my mother's table. (As my mother boasted afterwards, it was a particularly good one: crisp on the outside, soft and squishy within.) Jane's response was rapturous. Soon everybody at Giovanni's had heard about the exotic dish and the next time my mother stopped off for a cappuccino on her way to the beach she was overwhelmed with requests for the recipe. The interest of some people was genuinely culinary, while others were just pleased to talk of something other than the topless issue which was dominating conversation that year.

The first person to go topless in Torre Saracena was a French girl called Yvette in 1970. It caused quite a stir but at the time nobody had the nerve to follow her example – much as they might have wanted to. Over the years, however, the trend established itself and bare breasts ceased to be a novelty and became the norm. Early pioneers were young, confident and perfectly formed. Later it became more democratic and breasts ran a cheerful gamut from pubescent buds to mature mammaries of the more relaxed kind. And then in 1979, young misfits from Naples' backstreet drug culture arrived, pitching their patched bivouacs down the far end of the beach where serrated drifts of rock met the butt of the headland. They were predominantly male and they were all into sunbathing naked.

It was the arrival of these undesirable, unsavoury nudists that brought Torre Saracena's long-simmering outrage over the topless question to the surface. It was railed against in the shops, the marketplace, in the back room of Giovanni's bar. Even Brunetto il Piccolo thought things had gone too far. Some among the summer crowd were sympathetic to their views but most held that the village had no right to complain. After all, hadn't 'foreigners' saved them from virtual starvation, transformed the economy and put the town on the map? If Torre Saracena wanted to be the tourist resort of its dreams, it had to accept that moving with the times was the price it had to pay.

This attitude appalled my mother. Although not offended by the topless trend herself (the day would come when she, too, discreetly jettisoned her bra), she sympathised with the local people's disgust and totally endorsed their right to express it. But she was as shocked as everyone else when the anger stopped being merely mutterings and erupted into action of the ugliest kind.

It happened at about three o'clock on a mid-week afternoon, a dead hour on the beach when everyone over the age of 25 is struck with acute post-sandwich lethargy. My mother was playing Scrabble under Jane's umbrella. (She refused to pay Leone's prices for umbrella rental and carried her own portable shade, a Lilliputian affair barely large enough for one person to get a head under.) The other players were Jane, Massimiliano, a writer from Verona, and his pretty, much younger wife, Laura. They were arguing over my mother's word 'zarf' – which would have netted her a load of points – when somebody suddenly shouted, '*Porco dio!* Look over there!'

The tone of alarm instantly roused people from their stupor. Rising from towels and deckchairs they blinked in disbelief at the twenty or so village men marching purposefully towards them from the new port. They were fully dressed, even down to socks and shoes, and carried an impressive array of chains, clubs, metal bars and heavy leather belts. Everybody knew immediately that they had come about the half-naked bathers. There was a heart-stopping moment when no one could move, followed by an explosion of frantic activity as women everywhere dived for their bras. In the midst of this confusion Massimiliano leapt to his feet. '*Fascisti tutti quanti!*' he bellowed, shaking a furious fist. He then went on to proclaim that his father had fought with the Resistance during the war and he himself would never submit to the intimidation of thugs. As a matter of principle, therefore, and regardless of what anybody else might do, his own wife was definitely not going to cover up.

Massimiliano was a striking man. Over six feet tall, he had the hawklike profile of an American Indian and a deep, barrel-chested torso awkwardly supported on long, stiff spindly legs. Recognising several familiar faces among the mob – including that of the barber who regularly trimmed his hair – he began flailing his arms and yelling invectives. At which point a chain-swinging group closed in on Jane's umbrella. Laura shrank back at their approach covering her small, girlish breasts with her hands. Bella threw herself sobbing into my mother's arms. Massimiliano was seized, slapped around a bit, then given a shove and sent sprawling. Finding their voices, Jane and my mother begged him to give way before anyone got seriously hurt. Still shouting and gesticulating, he allowed Laura to pull on a T-shirt. He was very concerned that he should not be thought cowardly. In fact, for weeks afterwards he was still making sure that people knew he had only capitulated for the sake of the women and girls.

The druggy Neapolitan youths got much more of a trouncing. As matters were dealt with in the same way where they came from, however, it did not really take them by surprise. There was a token show of resistance, after which they quickly put their trunks back on.

But the foreign community was deeply shaken, wandering in stunned disarray like people who had narrowly escaped massacre by marauding barbarians. This was followed by a spontaneous drift up to Leone's (the entire family had made themselves scarce when the mob arrived), where a rowdy meeting soon got underway. Among those who took the floor were Massimiliano, Jane and a lawyer from Rome called Enrico. Eventually things quietened sufficiently to allow coherent debate, and it was decided to make a formal protest to the mayor the same evening. Even my mother agreed to take part. Like everyone else she was in shock. The experience had made her understand the full extent to which violence can render even the most capable person powerless.

While all this was happening someone decided to inform the media. As a result the incident was covered on the TV and radio news and by early evening the village was swarming with reporters. Bitterly disappointed to have missed the pictures – the combination of bare breasts and cudgels being irresistible stuff – pressmen were feverishly running around interviewing everyone.

Most popular were attractive young females, especially if well endowed, who were urged to give provocative views (and a photo opportunity) on the rights and wrongs of topless display.

The meeting with the mayor was scheduled for 8 p.m., and at 8 p.m. precisely the protest delegation trooped into the Town Hall. The mayor had not yet arrived, but representatives of the Saracenesi had. Emotions were running high and when the two sides met the room exploded into uproar. Accusations and recriminations were hurled across the cultural divide. For almost an hour there was uninterrupted shrieking and screaming, during which nobody even tried to listen to what anybody else was saying. At last, flanked by council dignitaries, the mayor made his solemn entrance. There was a momentary hush as they pushed through the throng and took up positions beneath a painting of Pope John XXIII at the far end of the hall. Then it all erupted again.

The chosen spokesperson for the outsider community was the lawyer, Enrico. His droning, repetitive deposition bled the episode of all drama and seemed to go on for hours. The villagers had no elected representative. Testimonies were given either individually or in tearful wailing choruses. They spoke in outrage and distress of their children being exposed to influences they disapproved of profoundly. They said that the beach, an inextricable part of their life, had become a place the village women no longer felt comfortable walking. They expressed the community's deep offence at people trailing up from the sea and wandering their streets semi-nude.

By 10.30 it was all over. The village women hurried home, the men lingered on the Town Hall steps to talk and smoke. The outsiders, in small, muttering groups, pushed through the jostling crowds on the bridge hoping to reach Giovanni's bar before it closed. Massimiliano said sourly that if it had not been for the presence of the press none of the councillors would have bothered to turn up. He also warned that in an hour the whole village would know exactly who had taken part in the protest to the mayor.

'We can all expect to be ostracised,' he said, adding darkly, 'if not worse.'

By this time my mother was extremely unhappy. Except for the thuggery on the beach, her sympathies lay with the locals. In her opinion the fact that they profited from tourism in no way invalidated their right to demand respect for their traditions and way of life. As she said to Jane, 'If I rent my house for a few months, I still expect the people not to deface the family photos or have orgies on the back lawn.' More than anything, she was dreading having to face Signora Lucia and her husband, Gaetano. It seemed to her that all the pleasure she had derived from their friendship, all the good feeling and mutual esteem, was now lost forever.

She did not join the others at the bar. Instead she went home and relieved the teenage girl who was babysitting for Bella. Then she made herself a cup of tea and, heavy-hearted, tried to read. Just before midnight there was a knock on the door. The noise made her jump, yet at the same time she realised she had been half-expecting it. For a moment distress at all she wanted to say but couldn't almost stopped her from answering. When she opened the door she found Gaetano smiling broadly at her. As usual where my mother was concerned, communication proved no problem. He made a short speech and then thrust a bowl of perfect tomatoes into her hands. She understood nothing except the most important thing – that her neighbours were reassuring her that she was exempt from their condemnation. Eyes pricking with grateful tears my mother did not even try to use words. She just hugged him.

But the topless controversy was not over yet. Although bikini tops made a resentful reappearance, the issue continued to fascinate the Italian press. Eventually an old judge from Rome gave his venerable opinion. It was all a question of aesthetics, he said. If a body was not a pretty sight then there was no question but it should be covered up. If the flesh was young, firm and pleasing to the eye, however – well, that was another matter altogether.

Pasta alla checca

Gaetano's tomatoes were sweet and succulent. My mother used them to make that genius combination of tomatoes, mozzarella and basil called a *Caprese*. *Pasta alla Checca*, eaten everywhere during the summer, is simply pasta served with a *Caprese* salad as sauce.

Feeds 4 as a main course

800 g (1lb 12 oz) penne rigati
2 fist-sized mozzarella, chopped into walnut-sized dice
500 g (1lb 2 oz) firm, ripe tomatoes, chopped into walnut-sized dice
Extra virgin olive oil
Big bunch of fresh basil
Salt and pepper

Cook the pasta in a large pot of boiling salted water and until al dente (should have a slight resistance when biting into it, but not a hard centre). Meanwhile mix the tomatoes and mozzarella in a bowl, add olive oil and season with salt and pepper. When the pasta is ready, drain, and stir in the tomatoes and mozzarella. Add the basil – torn into rough pieces, not chopped – and serve. Keep a bottle of extra virgin olive oil on the table for those who want to add more.

Chapter Fifteen

FABRIZIO

Every year property values in Torre Saracena took another leap. Such was the demand that even the meanest and dankest of places commanded an outrageous price. With this incentive the villagers continued the enthusiastic selling-off of their ancestral homes, decamping to the new jerry-built apartment blocks that continued to mushroom all over the sandy wastes of Saracena Mare. And inevitably the service shops followed: the hardware shop, the ironmonger's, the electrical supplier and the chemist. The chemist swapped a cracked stone floor and ancient medicine bottles shrouded in dust for marble, plate glass and smart displays of sunglasses and cosmetics. Even Salvatore, ousted by a steep rent increase, found much larger and cheaper premises from which to sell his cakes and pastries. He quickly became very rich in this new location and, circumventing planning permission, built what he described as 'the house of an English lord' in the back-lying hills.

Cheap pizzerias opened on Saracena Mare's main street and there was a proliferation of chrome-shiny bars complete with jukeboxes and pinball machines. Tourism had also given it three hotels. Large, imposing, with decorative tiled foyers and jutting balconies, they straddled the new town's seafront like cruise liners stranded by the tide. Of all the changes the villagers had seen, these hotels were among the most welcome. Not only did they provide many people with work, but they were also venues where important family occasions like weddings and christenings could at last be celebrated in appropriate style.

For Luca and his friends, Saracena Mare with its tackiness and bustle was where the 'real' Saracenesi children lived; the tough ones, the ones who knew what it was all about. This view was consolidated when Luca made friends with Fabrizio the summer they both turned twelve. Small, skinny and full of spunk, Fabrizio was a *fico*, a *capo*, a cool dude, the village equivalent of a streetwise city kid. He knew all the ins and outs of his environment and just how to manipulate it to the best of his advantage. He knew about the sea and fishing, about caves and driftwood, about the rumoured sites of buried treasure. He also knew how to pinch fruit from under a farmer's nose, haggle a price with the shrewdest market trader and how to come out on top in any confrontational situation. And as far as stealing freshly baked *cornetti* from Salvatore's at five in the morning – well, he was simply the best. Where the outsider children were concerned, however, it was the day Luca got into trouble with Peppino that Fabrizio's reputation was really made.

Peppino was not popular with any of the children, local or otherwise. Firstly, he was bad-tempered. Secondly, his bar tables had been inching ever further into the Piazza and eroding their play area. This issue provoked strong feelings on both sides. The children stood up for their right to romp, Peppino for his right not to have his business disturbed. On the afternoon in question he was blustering about trying to break up a hot game of football. Not only did the children ignore him, but at a certain point Luca fielded a powerful header which whizzed across the Piazza, bounced off a wall and missed Peppino's large, hairy ear by a whistling millimetre.

Peppino did not like children but he made an exception for Luca. Along with everyone else he had been seduced by Luca's winning brand of urchin charm. On this occasion, however, he was not beguiled. Bellowing with rage, he grabbed a broom and gave chase, determined to give Luca a sound beating. But Peppino was outclassed from the start. It took no time at all for a gleeful Luca to run his overweight, chain-smoking, 60-year-old pursuer into the ground. The addition of insult to near injury was more than Peppino could bear.

'Right, you grinning little bastard,' he gasped, shaking his fist. 'Now you're really in for it! Just wait and see!'

Storming out of the Piazza he returned minutes later with two strapping youths. The deal, as they later explained, was free beers in exchange for 'sorting the little shit out'. This they commenced to do, grabbing Luca by his T-shirt and a fistful of tangled, shoulder-length hair. Luca responded by transforming himself into a Catherine wheel of whirling limbs as he struggled to break free. The other children gathered around shrieking and aiming kicks at the big lads' knees. Luca managed to spit at one of them, for which he received a painful prod in the centre of his bony chest.

It was then that Fabrizio, who was shorter than Luca and just as scrawny, sprang to the fore. Bristling with theatrical bravado he squared narrow 12-year-old shoulders and said in the husky, uncertain falsetto of a voice about to break, 'Let my friend go! I'm the man you settle any problems with, OK? But not here, at Saracena Mare. Meet me in the Hotel Sirenella car park at ten tomorrow morning and I'll wipe the floor with both of you. Single-handed!'

Fabrizio issued his challenge knowing it would not be taken up. It was simply a brilliant psychological ploy. Casting himself in the role of pint-sized hero, Fabrizio made the youths look like cowardly bullies – which they were, of course. His bold and fearless stance also made them look ridiculous, leaving them with no alternative but to extricate themselves from the embarrassing situation as quickly as possible. It was a hard exit to make. Assuming expressions of bored indifference, they slouched off, followed by a chorus of whistles and boos.

Peppino, beside himself, climbed onto a bench. Still brandishing the broom, he announced that he was calling the police and when they arrived all under-fifteens who were still in the Piazza would be immediately arrested. But the children were far too busy lionising their new champion to pay Peppino's rantings any attention. To a jubilant chant of 'Fa-bri-zio! Fa-bri-zio! Fa-bri-zio!' they slapped his back, ruffled his hair and swept him off to be fêted with sneaked cigarettes and beer.

Fabrizio was brave, funny, cunning and smart. He was into fast motorbikes and rock and roll and was forever asking questions about big city life. In return he taught his outsider friends the 'cool' Saracena ways, the hows and whys of his closed and ancient world. On one occasion he borrowed a rowing boat and took Luca and Tammy down the coast to a cave where a debauched Roman emperor had staged lavish orgies. It was enormous, as echoing and cavernous as the belly of Jonah's whale. At the top of a high, banked tier of broken rock was a recess – a cave within a cave – just big enough for the three of them to stand up in. It was his special place, his refuge when he needed to be alone. Once, he said, he had even spent the night there. Luca and Tammy were awestruck at his courage. The air, sharp and dank, felt like ghosts' breath on the skin. The hollow silence echoed with the sucking and swirling of water deep in black-throated crevices far below.

When they re-emerged Fabrizio found a small pink shell shaped like a perfect heart. He gave it to Tammy and asked if she would be his girlfriend. Tammy was delighted with the shell (which she threaded on a string and wore as a necklace for the rest of the summer) but declined to be his girlfriend.

'Why not?' Fabrizio asked, more puzzled than hurt.

'Because if I was your girlfriend we'd have to kiss and the thought of kissing anybody makes me sick,' she replied.

Fabrizio's father was a fisherman and the family were very poor. They were also strict and Fabrizio was regularly beaten, mostly by his mother who was the most severe. She thrashed him with a belt, a cane carpet beater and, on more than one occasion, broke a plate over his head. Of all the punishments, the worst was having to kneel on dried chickpeas in front of a picture of the Virgin Mary.

'*Gesu mio!*' she would cry as she leaned on his shoulders to force him down. 'Tell me what I did to be punished with a son like this!'

Fabrizio was caught between two cultures: the one he was born into and the 'foreign' culture to which he yearned to belong. When the summer season ended, when his outsider friends departed, when the streets emptied and the shutters came down, then all that was left was the Big Void. No more fun, no more action.

Marijuana had been around since the Big Bang but now the heroin scourge sweeping Italy had a foothold in the village too. Fabrizio started taking the drug in his thirteenth year. In March 1982 – on a winding and treacherous road known locally as the *Strada Maledetta* ('the cursed road') because of the number of lives it claimed each year – the car in which he was travelling collided with a lorry. It was late afternoon, a week after his fourteenth birthday. He was on his way to an appointment with a pusher with two older boys. All three were killed on impact.

Grief at the deaths was shared by the whole village. It was a *lutto cittadino*, a collective tragedy. Everybody, local officials and dignitaries included, turned out for the funeral. The women wore the timeless black dresses and veils of deep mourning. The men wore dark ill-fitting suits, many twenty, thirty, forty years out of date. In the flower-filled church the smell of mothballs rising from the congregation's clothing competed with that of wax and incense.

About ten of Fabrizio's Roman friends took the day off school to come down for the funeral. They participated from the sidelines, aware that for many they represented the road to perdition along which Fabrizio had lost his way. But they had also loved him and they knew how much he would have wanted their presence, not only to mourn his untimely passing, but to stand witness to all his unfulfilled hopes and dreams. To remember the vision of the adventurous, unfettered world citizen he was so impatient to become.

Fabrizio was the only one of the three teenagers in a fit state to be viewed. In fact, he was almost unmarked. Only a small hole on his temple indicated where a piece of metal had pierced his skull. For several hours before the service friends and relatives visited the open coffin set in a side chapel to pay their last respects. Luca had never seen a corpse before and was deeply affected. To him, his friend looked not so much asleep, as he had hoped, but like a skilfully crafted waxwork model of himself. The glossy, crisply curling eyelashes, the composed lips, the olive smoothness of his still hairless skin, gave him an unreal perfection that hadn't been there in life.

Unable to pay for new clothes on top of the funeral costs, Fabrizio's family had dressed him in a maroon suit with the wide, flapping lapels fashionable in the seventies. Probably made for his father or an uncle, it had been worn only for important occasions. In the eyes of his family and the village it dignified him. To his friends, however, it was unbearably humiliating and sad. Getting rid of Fabrizio's jeans and T-shirt, his *fico* baseball jacket, was the ultimate denial of everything he held himself to be.

It was three miles from the church to the cemetery. The route took the cortège down winding streets of the old village, through Saracena Mare, past rows of greenhouses fluttering silvery tatters of polythene at traffic hurtling along the dusty main road. It was a long, painful and stumbling Via Dolorosa. Every now and then the procession halted to allow a fresh relay of men to shoulder the coffins. When Luca and other outsider friends stepped forward nobody objected. Grateful to be allowed to play their part, they carried Fabrizio on the last lap of the journey to his final resting place.

Once at the cemetery, grief exploded with the desperate passion that characterises funerals in Italy's south. Weeping women waving *santini* (holy pictures) and heavy metal crosses invoked the intervention of the Madonna, San Rocco and San Leone and all the other blessed saints. Relatives wailed, beat their breasts, collapsed swooning in each other's arms. In a frenzy of desolation, the brother of one of the older boys threw himself on the coffin waiting to be interred. Kicking, pummelling and clawing the veneered lid, he begged God in His mercy to bring his brother back to life. The mayor was trying to deliver the eulogy but it was like shouting into a gale, his words lost to the maelstrom raging about him. Eventually he gave up and, together with the priest, went to help those attempting to prise the distraught youth off the coffin.

When it was all over, Luca and his friends picked wild flowers and trudged another three miles to lay them on the spot where the accident had occurred. It was already a shrine; the grass verge was banked high with floral tributes and photographs of the three boys were nailed to the nearest tree. The picture of Fabrizio had been taken when he was about twelve, the year he and Luca became friends. He looked very solemn and well behaved, his hair neatly brushed and the impudence of his dark eyes blanked out by the flash of the camera. Cigarettes were lit and Tammy, voice choking with tears, recited a rude ditty he'd taught her one stormy summer afternoon. Moments of silence were interspersed with the telling of Fabrizio stories and someone handed round the Etruscan coin Fabrizio had given him in exchange for a Swiss Army penknife.

But despite everything, despite the open coffin, the scene at the cemetery, the flowers piled around the photograph pinned to the tree, they found it hard to believe Fabrizio was really dead. To accept that meant accepting that their own existence was a fragile reality that a whim of fate might snatch away at any moment.

Instead of going back to the village they went to the beach. Leone's and Tullio's establishments were closed and stray dogs with matted coats and scabby sores watched warily from lairs hidden in the dunes. At the sight of the great expanse of glittering winter sea, the sharp March breeze blowing hard in their faces, sadness and confusion evaporated. In its place came an explosion of energy and joy. With wild, whooping cries they threw off their jackets and ran themselves ragged in a leaping, laughing dance that celebrated the raw life force animating them.

When the time came to leave, however, the euphoria left them again. For it hit them at last that death is real, final, and nothing can change that. Accepting this painful truth was what finally enabled some of them to cry. Then Luca foraged around for a suitable stick and, each taking a letter, they wrote *CIAO FABRIZIO* in four-foot-high capitals in the cold, damp sand.

Pizza, prosciutto e fichi

After Salvatore's move to Saracena Mare, the only place in the old town selling trays of pizza was Vapo Forno, the village bakery. It belonged, as did Bar Sole, to the family of Stella's dour friend, Maria Pia. Unlike Giovanni, who reserved his antipathy for outsiders, Maria Pia and her two sisters disliked their fellow townsfolk too. The shop area at the front of the cavernous old bakery was so begrudgingly small, all you needed was four plump matrons to create a squeeze. Driven by hunger Luca and his friends managed to pack themselves in, however. But all they found was a tray of *pizza bianca* (white pizza) which a tight-lipped Maria Pia cut into careless squares. It was cold, dry and the coarse-grained sea salt embedded in the crust scratched their mouths. It bore no resemblance to Salvatore's far superior version which we used as the basis for a favourite summer treat: *pizza, prosciutto e fichi*. In this recipe the warm saltiness of the pizza is deliciously counterbalanced by the sweetness of the Parma ham and the ripe, juicy figs.

Quantities optional

Fresh ready-made white pizza
Parma ham
Ripe, juicy figs

To make the pizza

500 g (1lb 2 oz) strong flour
1 sachet dried yeast dissolved according to packet
instructions
3 pinches of fine salt
coarse grained salt for scattering on top
Olive oil
Fresh rosemary

Make a hole in the mound of flour, add the dissolved yeast and fine salt. Knead vigorously for about 10 minutes, adding more hot water if necessary. Cover the dough ball with a damp cloth and leave to rise for 2 hours. Starting from the centre press dough into an oiled oven tray, leaving an inch of unpressed border (which will puff up). Sprinkle with coarse grained salt, rosemary leaves and a generous slurping of olive oil. Cook for 20–25 minutes in a preheated oven (190 °C/ 375 °F/ Gas Mark 5).

When ready to serve, divide the pizza into portions, cut open, and fill generously with parma ham and sliced figs.

Chapter Sixteen

THE PIRATES AND THE MAFIA

The tree outside Giovanni's was Torre Saracena's only tree of consequence. It was also the only tree the old town proper had. Situated outside Giovanni's and on the opposite side of the Piazza to my mother's flat, it crowned the broad steps that forked to the Belvedere on the left and to the beach on the right. Generations of children had climbed its branches, generations of old men had enjoyed its shade. As, indeed, did those of us who for years now gathered at the tables Pina and her sister crammed beneath it. It was 'The Tree'. A village landmark. A presence of civic status.

Arboreally speaking it was not impressive, however. Eighty to a hundred and thirty years old (depending on who you were listening to), it was barely sixteen feet high and about half as wide. Its knotted branches were crabbed and graceless and never produced anything approaching luxuriant foliage. Like many of the older villagers, it gave the impression of being stunted by poverty. Its trunk had a weary incline and was riven by a cleft so deep that in one place it was almost hollow. Etched deep in the rugged corrugations and battered folds of its thick, greyish bark was an imprint of Torre Saracena's own harsh story.

Then early one January morning in 1984 the unthinkable happened. Three men sent by the town council arrived to cut it down. The official reason was fungal disease. The more probable explanation was that it was old, unprepossessing and did not fit the image of a smart holiday resort the town was so anxious to cultivate. For 'smart holiday resort' was still what Torre Saracena aspired to become. To this end the council encouraged the proliferation of snazzy boutiques and the sort of takeaway roast chicken and pizza outlets found in towns and cities all over Italy. They were cheap and convenient and lots of people loved them. I refused to be tempted. If I wanted pizza then I walked to Salvatore's, now relocated in the new town, and feasted on his substantial slabs succulent with tomato and rich green olive oil.

Another aspect of Torre Saracena's makeover was to recreate bits of itself as picturesque parody. This was what happened when a small courtyard of buildings located through an arch off the main street was converted into holiday flatlets. It was the first-ever large-scale property redevelopment in the old town and as such attracted everybody's interest. I was shown round at an early stage by Andrea (the man I was forever chasing to repair my mother's leaking roof) who was doing the plastering. 'This is no ordinary conversion,' he told me proudly. 'Here we're talking class and refinement. It'll show the world that Torre Saracena can compete with Positano any day.'

The end result was awful: eight featureless, box-like flats where the old terracotta floors had been replaced by shiny tiles in a bathroom shade of pale blue. The central courtyard was transformed into a Disney stage set complete with a fake well, fancy iron wall lamps and a 'medieval' mural depicting ferocious pirates raiding villages along the coast. Villagers gave it unreserved approval, as did the coachloads of day-trippers who jostled cameras to get the best-angled shots.

Pirates were a part of its history that Torre Saracena enjoyed owning. The days when the community had lived in terror of an attack were long gone and the story could now be retold – as it was in the mural – with a romantic and swashbuckling glamour. There were events in the more recent past, however, that still carried such trauma they were never mentioned. It was only the silent queues at the post office on the days that the war 'disability' pensions were paid out which still bore testimony to a shame everyone wanted to forget.

The Allied assault on southern Italy began in 1943 and included French colonial troops commanded by officers of the French Foreign Legion. Recruited mostly from Senegal and Morocco, their brutality was such they were feared even more than the Germans. This was because whenever they took a town or village a wholesale rape of the population took place. In the spring of 1944 all the females of six villages in the vicinity of Torre Saracena suffered that fate. And it was not only women who were ravished. In one of the villages, deciding that fifty women were not sufficient for their needs, the soldiers went on to rape children and old men too.

When the French colonial troops arrived in Torre Saracena, the mayor of the time, wearing his ceremonial sash of office and flanked by members of the council, was waiting in the Piazza to greet them. He hoped that by offering an immediate and unconditional surrender the village would avoid the terrible fate of its neighbours. Unfortunately this was not to be. The first person to be raped was the mayor himself, publicly and on the very spot he had been standing. Then came the turn of the rest of the council. After that the soldiers went on a 24-hour rampage during which they raped every female they could lay their hands on. Brunetto il Piccolo told Lorenzo that one girl, 12 when she was repeatedly raped along with her mother, did not speak again for 15 years. And when she eventually found her voice again – in the hush of a Sunday church service – it was to scream, 'Jesus is a fucking bastard!'

One of the dignitaries of the time, a giant of a man with an enormous belly and a lozenge-shaped, hairless head was now one of the old men who spent their days sitting around Giovanni's. An early riser, he was already at the bar on the day the men arrived just before seven to cut down the tree. According to his testimony, it took less than twenty minutes to sever the trunk. But digging out the stump and roots was a bloody battle and took the best part of three hours. First there was the breaking up of the surrounding stone and concrete, then the men had to gouge out what was left of the tree. When it was done it left a gaping hole the size of a small bomb crater. This brutal amputation left the Piazza disfigured and bereft. Shocked villagers stood around staring at the hole as though it was a corpse, the victim of a knifing or hit-and-run driver. The old dignitary in particular was very distressed; so much so that he broke down in tears.

'They should never have done this!' he raged. 'The people should have been consulted. There should have been a referendum. Mark my words, cutting down this tree will bring great misfortune on us all.'

To Billy, the removal of the tree was devastating, the latest in a long line of inconsolable losses. Only an hour earlier he had looked out of his window to see work starting on the first of five villas that would be built on the steep slope flanking the main steps to the beach. In a few months the scrubby sweep, home to clumps of spiky rosemary and wild garlic, would be lost to bricks and concrete. There would be terrace parties and noisy barbecues. The world he had come to Torre Saracena to escape was squatting on his doorstep.

A few weeks later he packed his few belongings and left for Rome. For a while he lived with Stella, then moved to a quiet apartment overlooking the magical melancholy of the neglected botanical gardens. The village was sad to lose him and there was much regretful sighing whenever his name came up. Nobody would believe he had left because of the tree, however. As old Giovanni said, 'Whatever happens here, whatever the changes, Billy's a Saracenese now. The village is in his blood. He'll be back before the year is out, just wait and see.' But he wasn't. Three years passed before he returned for a visit that lasted just a few days.

Giovanni was one of the few who was pleased that the tree was gone. He enjoyed the controversy and he enjoyed anticipating the upset it would cause the outsiders when they arrived at Easter. He agreed with the council: the tree was rotten with disease and like all things diseased it had to go. Berto the Fascist, recently diagnosed diabetic, took this extremely personally.

'Diseased like me, you mean, don't you?' he shouted during a heated exchange on the subject. When Giovanni merely cackled, Berto slammed his cards on the table and stormed out.

The old dignitary, roused from years of almost terminal apathy by his strong feelings on the matter, took Berto's side. Cutting down the tree was an outrage, he said, repeating his warning that it would bring misfortune on them all.

'Misfortune for those foreigners who'll get sunstroke,' Giovanni said gleefully. 'Not for me!'

Whether the tree had anything to do with it or not no one can say, but five days after making that remark Giovanni's wife died and a week later he followed her. It was a day like any other and he had spent most of it playing *scopone* in the back room of the bar. In the evening Pina's sister, Claretta, went over to cook his supper (a task they had been sharing since he became a widower). She made *pasta in brodo* followed by sautéed chicken livers and boiled spinach – none of which met with his approval. As she was leaving Giovanni reminded her to send her husband over to see about the disturbed reception he was getting on his TV set. When the husband arrived shortly afterwards, however, he got no answer to his knocks. He called the carpenter – who was in the middle of his own supper – and together they levered the door off its hinges. They found Giovanni dead in an armchair, his wife's voluminous white apron lovingly enfolded in his arms. According to Pina, the only thing ailing her father was a broken heart.

Giovanni was a tyrannical patriarch of the old order. Despite marriage and children of their own, his two middle-aged daughters had never managed to break free from his control. This was partly due to the fact that they had both worked for him since leaving school at the age of ten. In those days there was no espresso machine, of course, and apart from the odd bottle of grappa and aniseed liqueur, the only alcohol sold was local wine. Coffee was brewed on a gas ring in a large Neapolitan tin pot and served in small glasses. The girls spent much of their days carrying the bitter black brew to wherever the recipients were working. By the time they were in their mid-teens they were running the place. But although they were expected to do all the work, they were never allowed to make an independent decision. Pina said they weren't allowed to so much as pin a calendar on the wall without Giovanni's permission.

Pina and Claretta recounted this without rancour. That was what families were like in those days and you just accepted it. Nevertheless, when the bar reopened after the funeral the lightness of their manner contrasted with the black garb of their deep mourning. After all the years of meek obedience the bar was now theirs and they could do whatever they wanted with it. And – given Giovanni had also left a sizeable inheritance – what they wanted was nothing less than a complete makeover.

The work was carried out by a specialised firm brought in from Rome. It started at the end of February and was completed in time for the Easter influx. All the old fittings were ripped out. The narrow bar with its battered zinc top was replaced by a grand sweep of decoratively carved walnut. Behind it was erected a mirrored cabinet on which the sisters ranged bottles of Campari, Punt e Mes, Martini, Stock 84, Fernet Branca, Sambuca Molinari and so on. These were decoratively interspersed with miniature gondolas, pictures of saints and sprigs of artificial flowers. The floor was retiled in a smart dark green and a second cabinet for displaying chocolate and fancy biscuits was positioned on the opposite wall. There was also a new toilet – although it immediately acquired a permanent 'Out of Order' sign after someone left it dirty.

Finally the bar was officially named Bar Petroni (the family surname) and given an illuminated sign. 'Bar' was written in large, square, red capitals, 'Petroni' in a smaller, ornate blue script. Pina and Claretta were especially gratified by this. As Pina said, 'What sort of bar is it if it doesn't have a proper name on a proper sign?'

During the refurbishment the old men decamped to the Little Bar in the New Piazza. They grumbled a bit but on the whole accepted the disruption with stoical resignation. The trouble started after the work was finished and they were settling back into their old routine. For it was then that the sisters announced that they were leasing the back room to a rich Neapolitan. The pool table would go and there would be no more sitting around all day gossiping and playing cards. The place was to become a smart fish restaurant.

That somebody was after the back room was nothing new. It was a large, unexploited space in a prime position and people had been after it ever since Torre Saracena's Big Bang. Giovanni, indifferent to even the juiciest carrot, had always said no. Pina and Claretta, however, were considerably more mercenary. The Neapolitan (who drove a white Mercedes and whose squat fingers were weighted down with gold) was offering the kind of rent one got for a large apartment in a select quarter of Rome. As far as they were concerned it was time the back room was put to profitable use so they could settle down to becoming seriously wealthy.

The old men were outraged and hurt. Not only had they lost a boyhood friend, but they had been evicted from the patch they considered inalienably theirs. They retaliated by removing themselves once again to the Little Bar. More damningly they also decided to '*levare il saluto*' (withdraw their greeting). This meant that Pina and Claretta were publicly shunned by men who had been their father's buddies and customers for more than fifty years.

Torre Saracena was still a community that respected age and there was much sympathy for the old men's plight. Making money was one thing, people said, heartlessness was another. You don't boot grandfather out of the house to give his room to a rich lodger. Signora Lucia, exasperated because she now had her husband under her feet all day, was also incensed.

'If we can't respect the wishes of the dead then the world's a sorry place,' she snapped. 'Poor Giovanni must be turning in his grave!'

Pina and Claretta's response was to become tight-lipped, close-faced and unapproachable. Despite the rise of public opinion against them, and regardless of any second thoughts they might be having, they were determined not to be coerced. The impasse looked set to become a long-running feud when matters took an unexpected turn.

It was a few days after Easter. The rich Neapolitan was hosting a lunch party on the terrace of his rented seaview flat. About fifteen people – including several girls with dyed blonde hair, minimal dresses and lots of make-up – were sitting down to a meal prepared by the Filipino housekeeper and her husband. Then, just as the roasted sea bass with wild fennel was being served, a swarm of *carabinieri* armed with Beretta machine guns burst in. There was a riot of screaming and shouting during which the Neapolitan was handcuffed and dragged out. As, indeed, were most of his guests.

The incident caused a great furore. The streets leading to the flat on the Belvedere had been cleared for the operation, as had the Piazza where an armoured police van was waiting to cart the Neapolitan away. The incident was important enough to make the TV news that evening as well as commanding columns in the newspapers the next day. The rich Neapolitan who almost opened a restaurant in Giovanni's back room was revealed to be a high-ranking *camorrista* (Neapolitan mafioso) and was wanted for extortion, drug trafficking, kidnapping and murder. His presence would have meant protection rackets and shoot-outs. The village trembled at the thought of what it had escaped.

The sisters immediately let it be known that they had suspected he was dubious and had already decided not to do business with him. Furthermore, Pina's husband called on the old dignitary at home to tell him the family now agreed that leasing the back room to anyone was not a good idea. Pina and Claretta, he said, wanted nothing more than that things should continue just as they had when old Giovanni was alive.

The very next morning the old dignitary, hands gravely folded on large belly, was back in his usual chair greeting friends and watching the world going by. Claretta brought him coffee on a tray and for a few moments they exchanged pleasantries as though nothing untoward had ever happened. Not long afterwards Cosimo arrived, followed shortly by Berto the Fascist and Signora Lucia's husband, Gaetano. By the end of the afternoon all the old cronies were back in their habitual places.

Meanwhile the council had replaced the tree with a scrawny, waist-high sapling that survived barely a week before children trampled it down. The old dignitary, more convinced than ever that cutting down the old tree had precipitated their recent misfortunes, remonstrated with officials who mumbled about other priorities and did not seem concerned at all. At which point, accompanied by sons and grandsons, the old dignitary took off for the hills, returning with a vigorous specimen over six feet tall.

The planting, performed with fitting ceremony by the same sons and grandsons, was attended by a large appreciative crowd. In the speech he gave afterwards, the old dignitary said he hoped the new tree would usher in 'an era of ever-increasing prosperity and happiness'. Nobody present could doubt that at that moment, he himself was a most happy and satisfied man. And, according to his daughter, he continued to be happy and satisfied right up to the moment of his death two months later.

Spigola con finocchio selvatico

Helping out in the mafioso's kitchen on the day of the lunch party was Signora Lucia's cousin, Signora Franca. She arrived early the following morning in a lather of high-decibel excitement to tell all. I followed their conversation from the comfort of my bed, as I'm sure did everyone else in the vicinity. We learned that the 'arch criminal' sported a gold Rolex costing 'milioni di lire', that the women present were all 'malafemine' (one of whom obviously wasn't wearing knickers), and that the Filipino couple hadn't had a holiday for three years. We also learned that *Spigola con Finocchio Selvatico*, sea bass with wild fennel, was the main course on the menu. It made her salivate enviously, she said. Sea bass was an expensive luxury she couldn't afford.

Feeds 4

1 kg (2 lb 3 oz) sea bass, cleaned
1 large orange
1 clove garlic
Small bunch wild fennel (alternatively cultivated fennel with fronds)
Large glass white wine
4 tbsp extra virgin olive oil
Salt and pepper

Finely chop fennel, garlic, rind of half the orange and mix together. Wash and dry the fish and season inside and out. Stuff the fish with the fennel mixture. Pour the oil and 2 tbsp of the wine over the fish, place in an oiled baking pan and cook in a preheated oven (170 °C / 340 °F/ Gas Mark 3) for about 25 minutes. Baste every so often with a tbsp of wine. When done, remove the fish to a warm plate. Add the juice of the orange to the liquid in the pan, and reduce for a few minutes over a lively heat. Pour the sauce over the fish and serve.

Chapter Seventeen

ARENA ITALIA

The open-air cinema was called Arena Italia. Next door to the abandoned old school and overlooking the sea on the side of Saracena Mare, it was a place of such magical delight you went regardless of what film was showing. The floor was packed earth and gravel, the tiers of wooden seats were so rickety whole rows would often collapse, and the small, tattered screen suspended in mid-air resembled a ghostly windbreak. Mimmo, who had lost the fingers of his left hand fishing with dynamite, sold ice cream and *gassosa* from a wooden shack he had built in a corner at the back. It was a meagre living, especially because he was always giving credit and rarely recovered the money. The owner was a fat man called Signor Luigi. He wore his hair slicked back and brilliantined like a thirties' film star. Although more of a businessman than Mimmo, he let people in for free – especially pretty girls who smiled sweetly at him.

Going to Arena Italia was more than just going to the cinema, it was another community event. You took along food (the Saracenesi favoured thick courgette or potato omelettes stuffed between hefty slices of crusty bread) and a rug to snuggle under when night breezes blew in from the sea. The projectionist, the owner's eldest son, was a frustrated motorbike mechanic and his mind was not on the job. The film inevitably started out of focus and it took several minutes of the audience shouting *'fuoco'* before he got it right. After that the chances were it either broke, caught fire (watching hungry flames licking the corner of the screen was an enjoyable diversion in itself) or there would be the inevitable power cut. Sometimes only the sound went and the background rasp of crickets could be deafening. Interruptions lasted anything from a few minutes to an hour. Often the problem was insoluble, in which case everyone collected their refund and headed back to the Piazza.

In those days, Italian cinemas were graded into first, second and third screenings. (*Prima Visione* screened new releases which ran for a few months before passing into *Seconda Visione*. *Terza Visione* frequently showed erotic films, as well as those that had been around for years). Arena Italia belonged to the circuit of provincial summer cinemas which changed their programme daily and showed absolutely anything as long as they could get it cheap: ancient blockbusters such as *Ben Hur* and *The Ten Commandments*; Malatesta's muscle-men epics like *Fire Monsters Against the Son of Hercules*; the Godzilla series; films featuring the great Neapolitan comic Toto, and, every now and then, an almost up-to-date American release or spaghetti Western. Mostly, the films were vintage and the prints were scratched and sometimes had vital frames missing. But that was accepted. If you got bored or lost the thread, you could always gaze at stars the size of lanterns, the lights of fishing boats ranged in a stippled line along the black horizon, or the illuminated bustle of Saracena Mare far below.

Another bit of fun was the lizards that crawled back and forth over the screen, inevitably settling on the heroine's nose during a romantic close-up. As far as we were concerned, children throwing stones to send them skittering was an integral part of the entertainment. And there were always plenty of children no matter how unsuitable the film. The owner operated on the principle that a ticket was a ticket and never refused entry to anybody. (If a parent said no, or the child could not raise the cash, they would join the others crowded onto the balcony of the derelict old school where they watched for free). Once in, they talked and laughed throughout, ignoring all attempts to shut them up. In truth, however, they were no more disruptive than the adults. For at Arena Italia audience participation was loud, lively and constant. Heroes were cheered, villains booed and sexy scenes whistled and applauded.

Torre Saracena itself was a natural film set, especially at night when small, precarious street lamps recarved the village into a mysterious world of highlighted stone and impenetrable shadow. Over the years many films had been shot there, one professional, the rest amateur. Despite pretensions to artiness à la Andy Warhol they were essentially home movies and that was their charm. For me, the most memorable was a Flash Gordon thriller that Hans, a German friend of Jasper's, shot on one of the first-ever video cameras in 1973. Jasper starred as Flash Gordon, of course, Lorenzo played Dr Zarkov and

Jasper's number one fan, Elio, put a fish bowl over his head to become Emperor Ming.

Another character, borrowed from *A Hundred and One Dalmatians*, was Cruella de Ville, interpreted by the alcoholic daughter of a venerated English statesman. She had only one line – 'This champagne is undrinkable!' – but there was extensive footage of her being chauffeured around in a white Rolls-Royce she had borrowed from an aristocratic friend. The garbled plot centred on the kidnapping of twin princesses (Claudia and Tammy) and ended with Dale Arden (Stella) cooking everyone spaghetti. That it had an ending at all was an achievement, for when the actors saw the first rushes they were so impressed by the brilliance of their performances that they went off and celebrated for three days.

Another memorable film, also directed by Hans, was what could be described as underground porn. In one of the key scenes the character Aphrodite Rising, played by a 65-year-old grandmother, makes love to a tattooed sailor. She is naked but for a black velvet pillbox hat and sequinned veil. Like Cruella, Aphrodite was a titled Englishwoman who long ago decided she much preferred the Latin ways. Plain, dumpy, with arthritic feet, she was also a nymphomaniac of the most outrageous and self-publicising kind. On realising that the film would only be seen at private screenings in Germany, she had her prime moments converted into stills and distributed among all her friends. Shortly afterwards she spent three months in a wheelchair after being exposed to a powerful insecticide that left her temporarily paralysed. This mishap, however, did not cramp her style. Her account of erotic dallyings with a young doctor in a hospital cubicle was published in a *Penthouse*-type magazine.

The most prolific of Torre Saracena filmmakers was an American called Ralph. As a young man a family friend got him a job as a gofer on a John Huston film and playing director had been a hobby ever since. About 45 when he first arrived in 1970, he was short and effeminate, with sagging jowls and pale blue eyes rendered girlishly starry by exceptionally long, lustrous curly lashes. But it was his voice that was most striking. A languid falsetto, it turned each sentence into a fanciful aria of trills and warbles.

Contrary to first impressions, Ralph was neither a eunuch nor a homosexual. He was a thrice-divorced father with a succession of live-in girlfriends. But what sabotaged these relationships was a libidinous interest in very young girls. His first sight of my sister, Louise – who, with her slight figure and corkscrew curls looked no more than 14 – caused a near swoon.

'Look over there!' he gasped breathlessly in his sing-song drawl. 'Just who is that exquisite, dimple-cheeked nymph?'

'My sister-in-law,' growled Lorenzo, who was drinking beer with Jasper at the next table.

'Then tell her,' Ralph said unperturbed, 'that she has utterly enslaved me.'

Unfortunately for Louise this turned out to be true. His sly, simpering courtship followed her to London and lasted for two years.

Ralph's Saracena film debut told the story of two children (played by his daughter, Dee, and Claudia) who overcame a terror of the village Ugly Man by making friends with him. When it was finished he hired Arena Italia for a night and invited everyone to a screening. It was a gala occasion. Fairy lights had been strung around the perimeter and a trestle table at the back was jam-packed with bottles of the local white wine. After a welcoming speech – in which Ralph referred to the film as his little *capolavoro* (masterpiece) – the lights went out and the titles flashed up on the screen. Before anyone had a chance to read them, however, they began elongating and sliding off to one side as if an invisible vacuum cleaner was sucking them up. This was followed by a flurry of frantic flickering and then everything went black.

In the hour it took to sort out the technical hitch, the audience got stuck into the wine and Mimmo sold his entire reserve of popcorn. This meant that when the film restarted everyone was in a good mood and ready to enjoy themselves.

The first frame was a close-up of Dee, eyes screwed up against the sun, a big grin exposing engagingly gappy teeth. A voice piped up from the audience: 'That's me! Gosh, aren't I little and goofy-looking?'

Action then moved to the Piazza, at which point the Saracenesi in the audience became involved. It was the first time any of them had seen themselves or their town on moving film and every person, doorway and flight of stairs was greeted with shrieks of delighted recognition. Carlo, a man whose huge hooked nose and fearful squint landed him the part of the Ugly Man, became an immediate celebrity. Sitting bang in the centre of the front row, he leapt up when the film was over, bowing and waving as though the applause was meant for him alone. For days afterwards he walked around preening graciously as people slapped him on the back or called out 'Bravo, Carlo! Got your ticket to Hollywood yet?'

Ralph made at least one short film a summer, which meant all of us got a look in sooner or later as background extras if not actually playing a part. One of them starred nine-year-old Marcello as a child whose repressive home life was killing his spirit as well as making him physically ill. He regains health and happiness when sent to stay with an aunt who lives an eccentric life with eccentric friends in a wild coastal paradise. To everyone's amazement it was bought by RAI TV and shown on one of their children's programmes. Ralph was immensely proud and for a while fantasised about chucking in his lucrative travel business and going professional.

On the whole, however, his films had no artistic merit whatsoever. But that did not matter because collectively they formed a sort of animated photo album, a fancy dress record of the last fifteen years of Torre Saracena life. So when in 1985 the news came that Arena Italia was closing, the old-timers among us agreed there was only one way to mark its passing. We would club together and hire the cinema again to give all of Ralph's films one last nostalgic screening.

The fairy lights came out again, Ralph and his new girlfriend, a Chinese-American at least thirty years his junior, provided sparkling wine and Mimmo turned up to sell Coca-Cola and popcorn. The programme was interrupted by the usual technical problems – four times to be exact – and a side row of seats keeled over when a group of teenagers tried sitting on the backs. Lizards crawled over the screen, crickets rasped and the great black bowl of sky shimmered with billions of stars. And if the audience was quieter than usual it was simply because it is hard to talk with a lump in your throat. I certainly couldn't when Luca suddenly flashed on the screen, a toothy five-year-old grinning down from the branches of The Tree with a Superman emblem painted in vivid red and blue on his little bare chest.

Each film was a wistful parade: small children grown big, one's young self now older, lost friends, lost lovers, lost familiar faces. Sullen Tammy wrapped in her flag, Claudia performing her belly roll, Stella wearing bright striped trousers with her wild, serpentine locks still intact. Jasper, Ringo, Elio, Lorenzo, Massimiliano, Jane, Hilary, Louise and Bella. Even me. A gory ten minutes of Mob and junkie Nicole cleaning cuttlefish and octopus for a casserole. Moments briefly captured on celluloid now gone forever.

We saw the Emporio again before it became a jeweller's, the *latteria* (milk shop) before it became a boutique, the summer beach before it began to resemble a lido, Brunetto il Piccolo in faded pink shorts before he became a Big Business Man. The old Tree featured heavily, of course, and there was the odd glimpse of friends like Salvatore now affluently settled in Saracena Mare.

The last film (a silly piece about a young girl and witchcraft) had a sequence where the protagonist meets a mysterious gypsy woman in a bar. I ignored this so-called action, all my attention drawn to the hunched and exceedingly grumpy figure of Giovanni in the background. I was suddenly aware of how much I missed him. I missed his rude, irascible dignity. His loyalty to old friends and old ways. While the rest of the village sold itself piecemeal to the highest bidder, he remained that rare thing: a man without a price. Watching him glower into the camera was the only moment I actually shed a tear.

The reason Arena Italia closed was because the owner sold the land to a property developer. Its place was taken by an indoor cinema that had been incorporated on the ground floor of an apartment block built a couple of years earlier by the big car park (once the kids' battleground) behind the Town Hall. The flats were a luxury development for seasonal rental. The cinema was a soulless, echoing chamber with whitewashed concrete walls and tiers of hard seats with a beige plastic veneer. As the equipment was new, breakdowns were rare, but the films were still the same old mishmash of whatever the proprietor could get his hands on. But whereas Arena Italia had always been well attended regardless of the programme, the indoor cinema was rarely more than a quarter full. This was due partly to its chilly lack of allure and partly to expense. Prices had been radically revised and a ticket cost the same as for a cinema in the suburbs of Rome or Naples.

I had been to the indoor cinema only once and I hated it. I swore I would never go again, but I did. The occasion was a late September evening just a few weeks after the Arena Italia closed. It was my birthday. Lorenzo and the boys were elsewhere and I arrived at Giovanni's to find not a single person I could join for a drink. Each year the summer population of Torre Saracena ballooned to ever more monstrous proportions. There were few of the original crowd left and the cosy days when all the tables at Giovanni's were occupied by friends had long passed. Nevertheless, to be confronted by a sea of unfamiliar faces still took some getting used to. Furthermore, the fact that the evening was supposed to be special made it even more melancholy. It was in this mood that I took myself off to the despised indoor cinema just for something to do until bedtime.

Fortunately, the film they were showing that evening was one of my all-time favourites, Ettore Scola's *Una Giornata Particolare* (*A Special Day*). Made in 1977, it tells the story of an encounter between the wife of a working-class Fascist official (Sophia Loren) and a left-wing homosexual (Marcello Mastroianni) on the day of Hitler's visit to Rome in May 1938. As a downtrodden madonna, Sophia is radiantly beautiful even without make-up. Marcello (the inspiration for my son's name) is sensitivity and tortured idealism personified. It is sex and politics Italian-style and it works for me.

I arrived just as the film was starting. There were no hitches so it was only when the lights came on at the end that I saw that there were just two of us in the audience: myself and Brunetto il Piccolo. He was sitting across the aisle with an untouched carton of takeaway chicken in his lap. He asked me if I had enjoyed the film and I said yes. I asked if he had enjoyed the film and he said yes. I then asked after his wife, Helga, and he told me she had been admitted to hospital that morning with cancer of the colon.

'That's why I'm here,' he said. 'I couldn't bear to be at home without her.' And covering his face with his hands he began to weep.

Afterwards we sat on a bench in the New Piazza talking, something we had not done for years. After a while he said, 'Do you remember when I used to come by and take Marcello to the Arena Italia? Well, once, during *Toto, Peppino e la Malafemmina* he gave me the slip and climbed into the projectionist's booth. I would never have known except that at a certain point the film caught fire and the owner found Marcello dousing the projector with a bottle of beer he'd found in a corner. That son of his had left a six-year-old in charge while he nipped off to do a bit of courting. I never told you that, did I?'

Frittata di zucchine

Marcello was like his father; he hated eggs (the mention of a fried one, for instance, triggered a display of throat-clutching, face-contorting and pantomime retching). Luca and I, however, loved them. So on the occasions he and I went to Cinema Arena alone together, I followed the local example and took wedges of courgette omelette sandwiched between crusty bread.

Feeds 4

6 eggs
2 large courgettes
1 tbsp minced parsley
2–3 mint leaves
Extra virgin olive oil
Salt and pepper
Good crusty bread

Slice the courgettes and brown in the oil with a couple of tablespoons of water. Meanwhile beat the eggs lightly with the parsley, mint, salt and pepper. Pour the mixture over the courgettes and tip the frying pan in all directions to spread evenly. When the underside is cooked remove from heat. Place a plate over the pan and flip it over. Slide the frittata back into the pan and return to the heat for a couple more minutes to finish the uncooked side off.

Chapter Eighteen

LENA LA LADRA AND THE LAST YEAR

For many years Brunetto il Piccolo was responsible for the renting and winter maintenance of my mother's flat. In return for a modest retainer he undertook to supervise small repairs and ensure the place had a regular airing. It was an arrangement that worked well until he married, after which Helga and the cultivation of richer clients claimed most of his attention. From then on (with the exception of organising the seasonal let of which he took ten per cent) he did nothing and the place was left to moulder. Nagging and complaining produced little result and I was obliged to spend much time and energy pursuing elusive electricians, plumbers and roofers – now only interested in large-scale conversions – in a desperate attempt to stop the place crumbling into disrepair.

In 1979 the business of my mother's drainpipe brought things to a head. According to Arturo, the proprietor of the wine and gas canister shop across the Piazza, the position of the drainpipe meant that it channelled rainwater into his cupboard-sized storeroom located beneath our steps. Brunetto continually promised to find someone to see about the problem but never did. It became a long drawn-out saga in which nobody co-operated and everything was made as exasperating and difficult as possible. The issue finally culminated in Arturo threatening litigation and a dramatic confrontation between Brunetto and myself in the middle of the Piazza.

In truth, the confrontation was not so much dramatic as farcical. After accusing Brunetto of dereliction of duty and betrayal of friendship, I declared our business relationship over and demanded the return of my mother's key.

'Never!' Brunetto cried, outraged, jumping back. Then, first dangling the key in the air, he dropped it inside his shirt like a defiant coquette tucking a disputed valuable into her cleavage. What he had forgotten, however, was that his Hawaiian shirt (everybody's favourite fashion item that year) hung loose over his trousers. The key slipped in at the top and out of the bottom, bouncing on the ground and coming to a skittering halt right at my feet.

For the next two years we did not speak. In the traditional village manner we 'withdrew our greeting', coldly averting our heads when we passed in the street. Making up was altogether speedier – accomplished, in fact, in less than five minutes. It happened one morning when we were both shopping at Signora Rosalba's market stall. I dropped my purse, Brunetto picked it up. I thanked him and we exchanged a smile. We then discussed tomatoes, agreeing they were not only expensive but flavourless, too. It was as though the rift had never happened, as though things between us were exactly as they had been before. Unfortunately, this was not so. For by then my mother's property was securely in the greedy grasp of Lena la Ladra (Lena the Thief).

During our first conversation, Lena told me that she had just installed gold-plated taps in the bathroom of her Saracena Mare home. She also boasted about her pink satin sheets and said she worked, not from necessity, but because she had a *'mentalita moderna'* and liked meeting different people. She said that her husband – who was head clerk with a Naples import-export firm (and almost certainly bumped up his salary with shady black market deals) – told her every day that he wanted nothing more than to keep her like a pampered princess in the comfort of their elegant home.

She was in her late thirties then, a dumpy woman with blonde-streaked hair, green eye shadow and a foxy smile. When the *latteria* closed she took over the premises and turned it into a tasteless, overpriced boutique. But the real money was in property and that was where her ambitions lay.

On hearing of my bust-up with Brunetto, she lost no time in beckoning me into her festooned lair. I was offered a seat, a cigarette, and given a long speech on the subject of properly drawn up contracts, smooth efficiency and all round professionalism. If I went with her, she said, she would 'handle everything' and I would never have to worry about everyday problems again. It was a persuasive pitch and exactly what I wanted to hear. In my heart, however, I distrusted her from the start.

It was agreed that Lena would pay for any repairs – carried out mostly in the winter – for which she would be reimbursed from the seasonal rental. It was Lena's suggestion and ultimately revealed itself as a wily ruse. For the bills she presented (always with illegibly scrawled receipts to back them up) were so outrageously inflated that, added to her agency commission, the profit we made from renting the flat was negligible. This meant there was never the money to do the major work – roof, plumbing, radical rewiring – that was so badly needed. Walls were whitewashed, cracked tiles replaced and new cushion covers and bedspreads made from oddments of lace and fabric found in the second-hand clothes market. But in the end it was just cosmetic, like sticking plasters on the broken body of an accident victim.

As a result the flat became progressively burdensome and less of a pleasure. Louise, Bella and my mother came increasingly rarely and by the early eighties we too were spending July and August elsewhere. If I continued to visit regularly it was because there was always some problem that urgently needed putting right (with Lena the only way to get an honest bill was to organise the work myself).

In the February of 1987 the problem was warped window frames. It was overcast when I left Rome and by the time I arrived in Torre Saracena it had developed into a mean and blustery day. Shutters rattled, posters and black-edged obituary announcements flapped on walls, and below the town the sea pounded the dun-coloured beach with debris and spume. Although not yet midday the village was deserted. Except for Saverio, that is, who was wearing an outsized grey jacket and standing in the centre of the Piazza like an old soldier abandoned on parade.

The flat had been uninhabited (and unaired) for almost five months. The air was stale and fusty and the floor gritty with sand that had blown under the front door and through myriad cracks and fissures. Climbing the stairs to the upstairs room, I discovered the roof had broken its record and leaked abundantly in about fifteen places. The armchair and bed were still sodden and mildew was spreading across the tabletop like patchy green lichen. There were wet streaks down the walls, a particularly ugly orangey-brown patch had appeared above the sink in the kitchen alcove, and plaster flaking from the ceiling lay everywhere like slivers of dead skin. Worst of all, when I moved the heavy chopping board a colony of cockroaches – black, shiny and the size of fat dates – skittered everywhere.

Lena heard of my arrival from a woman who had been the only other passenger on the morning bus from the station. She came at once to find me sunk in dejection and defeat. Her own manner was brisk and cheerful. She told me that the way to make the money to fix the place up was to rent it for an entire year.

'And it just so happens I know the very people,' she said, flashing her crafty gold-toothed smile. 'Two businessmen from Naples are opening a piano bar in Via S. Leone and they're prepared to pay well for a convenient place to live.'

I reminded her that the Neapolitans we had rented to the previous summer had taken home an antique Indian wall hanging and the hinged mahogany mirror off the top of the chest of drawers.

'Ah,' she replied, 'but these are a different class of people. I've had dealings with them and can personally vouch for their character.'

We went together to the public phone and Lena waited while I called my mother in London to discuss the proposal. Neither of us set much store by Lena's character reference but agreed that, given the circumstances, it seemed the most sensible thing to do.

'Good!' said Lena with satisfaction when I told her. 'You've made the right decision. I will go immediately and arrange a meeting for tomorrow.'

Lena hurried to her red Fiat Uno parked behind the new church. I took myself off to the Belvedere. I sat on a bench and huddled into my coat, watching dark clouds heave thunderously over the turbulent grey sea. After a while an old woman came by dressed in a thin black dress and cardigan and balancing a cloth bundle on her head. She informed me she had been collecting medicinal herbs in the hills and proudly unwrapped her bounty for display. She gave me a bunch of tough hairy leaves and (in dialect that I still struggled to understand) instructed me on the making of a tisane to cure 'my intestinal ills'. I confessed it was not intestinal ills but financial ones that were most troubling me.

'Listen,' said the old woman, waving her hand dismissively. 'If you shit well, you live well – take it from me!' And at that she walked off chuckling.

Over the years Jasper's number one fan, Elio, had become a good friend. We nicknamed him 'L'Orso' (The Bear) because he was big and shambling, a name he bore with pride and gave to the bar he opened in 1980. L'Orso – an ex-repository for wine and oil – resembled a crypt or truncated tunnel and was so narrow it was standing room only. Despite the discomfort, however, it soon became a home from home. A place where a woman alone was protected from harassment, where messages were left, and where photographs of Torre Saracena's early habitués (particularly Jasper) covered the walls.

That evening L'Orso was empty and Elio, feet up on the bar, was eating roasted sunflower seeds and drinking Prosecco.

'Well, look who's here,' he said, pleased to see me though not at all surprised. 'What's the trouble this time?'

'Don't ask,' I replied gloomily, accepting the glass of dry, sparkling wine he offered. I told him my sorry tale of the leaking roof, cockroaches and Lena's Neapolitan rescue package.

The politics of survival in a small community are complex. One fundamental rule, however, is that you keep out of anything that doesn't directly involve you or your close family. After all, when existence depends on the exchange of favours, when the uncertainties of life mean you can never predict who you will need tomorrow, only the most foolish would risk antagonising anyone unnecessarily. I was deeply indebted therefore when, after listening to my account, Elio decided to break this cast-iron rule. More than indebted, in fact, I was deeply and eternally grateful. For Elio told me that the people Lena was setting me up with were nothing less than members of the Neapolitan Mafia, the fearsome Camorra.

Elio explained it like this. Since the scandal of Giovanni's back room, everybody was aware that racketeers were after a slice of Torre Saracena's tourist trade. All their efforts had been unsuccessful until my proposed tenants forced Signora Teresa's nephew, who had defaulted on gambling debts, to hand over the keys of the boutique he had just opened. With all apartments in the village either occupied or kept for seasonal rental, however, they now had the problem of finding somewhere to live. 'If you let them have your mother's flat, she'll never get it back,' Elio warned. 'Since the laws on second homes were changed after the last earthquake, all those *merdoni* have to do is declare they're homeless and that's that. You can't get them out even if they stop paying rent. Any contract Lena draws up is worthless – and she knows it!'

My first instinct was to find Lena and kill her. Instead I went to see her brother, Mario, our friend and the proprietor of La Torre in Saracena Mare. La Torre was the only really decent trattoria in the whole village. During the summer the large square room festooned with plastic vines was always full. That evening, there was only one customer, however, the fat priest, who sat in a corner, napkin tucked into the neck of his cassock, working his way through a mountainous platter of *fritto misto* and a litre jug of white wine. He looked up as I passed on my way to the kitchen.

'*Buona sera,*' he intoned, his pouched, heavy-lidded eyes glazed with gluttonous pleasure.

At first Mario assumed it was hunger that had brought me to his door. When I said I had come about something much more serious, we sat down together at the kitchen table. Without revealing my informant, of course, I related everything Elio had just told me. I also pointed out that my mother would not be the only one betrayed. By helping the Camorra get a foothold in the village Lena was nothing less than a traitor to the whole community. Mario was deeply shocked.

'I can only think my sister has gone mad,' he said, 'and I will go to see her straight away and tell her so.'

That night I slept badly. At 5.30 a.m. the street sweepers made a noisy arrival and by six I was hunched over a small pile of damp wood attempting to drum up a fire. In the grey light of early morning everything looked even shabbier and more dejected than it had the day before. I swept the floor, wiped the mould off the table, then stood at the window watching Pina open the bar and the Piazza slowly coming to life. At 7.30 a.m. Lena arrived, smartly dressed in a black skirt, bright red jacket and gold hoop earrings the size of coffee saucers. She looked worried but not overly so.

'Mario says that you're, you know… upset,' she said, giving the chair I offered her a fastidious brush. 'That's why I'm here. So we can discuss things and put your mind at rest.'

I had promised myself that whatever happened I would not lose my temper, but one look at her crafty face and I blew. Lena had no objection to being called the biggest liar and cheat ever. On the contrary, her coy, simpering shrug indicated she took it as rather a compliment. What did disturb her was my threat to tell the world of her villainy and ruin her reputation forever. She had been too crafty for her own good, I shrieked. Nobody would ever trust her with their property again. She was ruined, her business was '*tutto finito*'. As for her smart new office, well, she might just as well get rid of it because she would never need it again!

Lena beat her breast, wrung her hands and swore on Jesus, the Madonna and a whole constellation of saints that she too had been duped and taken in. It was a blow to her heart, she cried, that people could think a woman like herself, renowned for goodness and piety, would have truck with gangland criminals. These mendacious denials served only to stoke my fire. I was almost levitating with fury. Only when I found myself trying to smoke two cigarettes simultaneously did I realise it was time to calm down.

My mother came at Easter, her first visit for two years. The only one of her old friends still around was Romina. Romina had been married for many years to a Turkish diplomat whose fanatical jealousy had kept her prisoner in her own home. Since leaving him she had become a mildly eccentric wanderer of the world, dedicated to personal freedom and the art of t'ai chi. Both women found the level of noise and congestion often unbearable (that year's craze among the teenagers was driving motorbikes full throttle up and down the beach). My mother's escape was her tiny roof terrace. For Romina it was taking her battered old moped a couple of miles down the coast for an hour or so of solitude.

Romina always chose the same spot, a grassy cliff top just ten yards or so off the main road. Once there she would settle herself cross-legged and contemplate the view. Her favourite time was around four in the afternoon. On Easter Monday, however, she decided to go early, taking figs and peaches for a picnic lunch. She had been there barely ten minutes when a car suddenly swerved onto the verge and came to a screeching halt behind her. A man got out. He was short, thickset, in his fifties like her, with a square face and cropped, greying hair. As he walked slowly towards her she became transfixed by the menace in his staring eyes. Then he took his arm from behind his back and she saw the wooden club he was holding.

The first blow caught her on the shoulder, the second on the side of the head. He continued to beat her, methodically and without passion, until she blacked out. At which point he threw her over the edge of the cliff onto rocks that tumbled twenty feet to the cove below. Throughout the whole assault the man uttered not a single word. He wanted neither sex nor the money that Romina in her terror begged him to take. All he wanted, it seemed, was to kill her.

Miraculously Romina did not die. She regained consciousness on a flat jut of rock that fortuitously broke her fall. For about half an hour she just lay there, dizzy with pain and shock. Then, inch by inch, she dragged herself back up again. A passing motorist took her to hospital where her injuries were found to include extensive internal and external bruising, a fractured wrist and arm, and a shattered cheekbone. Her brother was summoned from Verona and my mother extended her stay by a week. Her only other visitors were the *carabinieri*. They came to see her three times and on each occasion their bullying manner of interrogation reduced her to hysterical tears. The questions focused not on gaining information that would help them identify her attacker, but on the reasons for her being alone in such an isolated spot. If they could not prove her a professional prostitute, then they would show she was a woman without morals, a shameless tart who by her loose behaviour had simply got what she was asking for.

My mother was deeply affected by the incident, as were we all. It was the sad culmination of our disenchantment, and it brought us to the decision to sell. By then there was a whole clutch of estate agents operating in the village and we gave them all the opportunity to find us the best buyer. I very much hoped it would be my old friend Brunetto. But it wasn't. It was Lena la Ladra, of course.

Bruschetta con fave

Mario's trattoria in Saracena Mare was the best in the village. Lorenzo and I had been regulars for several years before we discovered he was Lena La Ladra's brother. That this charming, honest and hard-working man was related to such a slippery character came as a shock. But by then he was a good friend so we couldn't hold it against him. The evening I burst in he was clearing the kitchen ready to close after the priest's departure. But seeing the state I was in he brought out a flask of wine, prepared a plate of garlic toast topped with broad bean puree, and let me rant on about his sister's perfidy until gone midnight.

Slices of casareccio bread (alternatively sourdough/
ciabatta)
Boiled and drained fave (broad beans)
Finely chopped wild fennel (alternatively cultivated
fennel with fronds)
Garlic
Extra virgin olive oil
Salt and pepper

Force the broad beans through a fine-mesh sieve. Toast the bread, drizzle with olive oil and rub generously with garlic. Pile on the broad bean puree, drizzle with more olive oil, season with the chopped fennel, salt and pepper and serve.

POSTSCRIPT

The news that we were selling the flat spread fast and even those who had regarded us with disapproval said they were sorry to see us go. Of these an old widow (who years before had berated me in front of Marcello and Luca for the shortness of my dress) told me I was a *brava signora* and invited me to her home for a coffee. Situated opposite the old church at the top of Via S. Leone, her apartment consisted of a single room dominated by an enormous iron-framed bed. There was a small balcony on which she grew lemon-scented geraniums and in 1953 a toilet and kitchenette had been added on the communal landing.

'Just imagine,' she said as she showed me around. 'I brought up three children and nursed a sick husband here. We lived like rabbits in a warren, yet a place like this is prime real estate now.'

She prepared coffee the Neapolitan way and served it in china cups delicately patterned in green and gold. We drank it sitting side by side on the edge of the bed, a crowned Virgin smiling down on us benignly cradling the Christ child in one arm and a sceptre of sprouting lilies in the other. Afterwards she took me on a tour of her cupboards and drawers, proudly displaying the sheets, towels, tablecloths and napkins that had been part of her trousseau sixty years before. The starched and immaculate linen, now threadbare in places and smelling of lavender and mothballs, evoked a lost world and drew her into reminiscence and melancholy.

'You are leaving at the right time, Signora,' she sighed, wiping away tears on the corner of her apron. 'We've got everything now, smart boutiques and restaurants and lots of money – but what does it mean? The best of Torre Saracena is gone forever.'

It was a sentiment echoed by the villagers who stopped me at every turn. Our greed blinded us, they said, but how can a community which had known nothing but hunger and deprivation be expected to value what it's got? It was the fault of the mayor and the town council. They should have drawn up plans to ensure we had economic growth without the destruction of our heritage. Remember, Signora, how it was when you first came? The quiet, the fishing boats, the empty beach? And what about the *festas* we once used to have? The candlelit processions? *Quelli erano bei tempi, vero*?

I could only agree and, clasping hands, lament with them. I felt not only sadness but also remorse. I had loved the village and I had taken from it but, like the other outsiders, I'd given little back. Yet nobody reproached me, for I had outlived notoriety and censure. By virtue of my long association I had become a mirror reflecting a happier and more innocent time. A witness to the heady optimism of Torre Saracena's early renaissance and the paradise it had lost.

Once the sale was concluded I did not return for two years. Torre Saracena figured prominently in my dreams, though; the beauty and menace, the passion and passivity, the sense of dark magic lurking in the tight maze of ancient streets. Eventually nostalgia got the better of me and I eagerly accepted when our Argentinian friends, almost the only survivors from the old days, offered me the use of their flat.

Although it felt strange to be 'homeless', staying in their apartment was a treat all of its own. Occupying the whole top floor of a tall, narrow house, it was unique in having escaped modernisation or decorative 'improvement'. The windows were small and set close to the floor, woodwork painted the traditional pale green had not seen a brush for over twenty years, the pink brick floor tiles were so worn many were concave. And from the tiny kitchen balcony I looked out over a tiered cascade of honeyed rooftops beyond which was the sea, a shimmering sliver on the horizon.

My welcome at Bar Petroni was almost formal. Wiping hands and smoothing down aprons, Pina and Claretta came from behind the bar for the ritual exchange of compliments and kisses. They looked tired and aged, which I attributed to the crisis caused by Pina's daughter going to live with a Dutch boyfriend in Holland. Signora Lucia, who was also selling up to move in with Maria Immaculata, now married in Saracena Mare, had told me all about it when I visited her.

'Home, work, home, work – it's all those women have ever known,' she said. 'And not a day's enjoyment from the money they've earned either. The children do what they please and don't want to know about the problems of the bar.'

Not that any of this was mentioned, of course. Instead we talked about the misfortunes of others, indicating with sighs and shrugs how well we understood the trials and tribulations women have to bear. I selected one of Salvatore's sugared doughnuts (now delivered in a box each morning by his handsome son) to eat with the cappuccino Pina offered me on the house. Watching her sprinkle chocolate on the froth I was suddenly taken back twenty years to our historic row over Louise and the broken beer glass – the only other occasion I had been accorded this generous gesture.

Later I went to the beach. It was a brilliant mid-November day and as I walked the sun's rays felt like hot hands pressing into my shoulders and back. The umbrellas had been packed away, as had the blue and white paddleboats holidaymakers could now hire. Once again, stray dogs nosed among the scrubby dunes and old men collected mussels from the rocks. I kicked off my shoes and let sand run like powdered silk through my bare toes. At the port a family of black cats baked on a wall of orange-streaked stone. I stopped to watch them, pondering their chances of survival in the age of computer games and video thrills. Improved, I decided.

The harbour was crowded with small yachts, among them an impressive two-tiered motor launch called Laura. Somebody was hard at work polishing the chrome and when he stood up to wave I recognised Marcello's ex-gang rival, Domenico.

'Not mine, it belongs to a rich Milanese,' he said ruefully when I started to congratulate him. 'I'm just paid to keep an eye on it.'

Domenico was now a plump young man with prematurely thinning hair. During the summer he worked as a waiter but his dream was to win the lottery like Signora Assunta's son, Leonardo, and open an American-style hamburger joint. At his invitation I joined him on deck, stretching out luxuriously on the cushions he hurried to provide. It was blissful: the lapping water gently rocking the boat, the fantasy of acquiring an instant golden tan. And while I sunbathed Domenico talked, a bit about a car he hoped to buy but mostly with moist-eyed nostalgia of the enchanted days when the boys of Torre Saracena waged war with their outsider counterparts.

'The gangs have gone,' he said. 'They're a thing of the past. But those will always be the best of times. Ask Marcello, he'll tell you.'

Leone's was already closed (he was so rich now he took his wife and youngest children on a two-month cruise every winter) so I went for lunch at Tullio's instead. Tullio was rumoured to be even richer than Leone with a fortune in excess of £3 million, most of it astutely invested in property. His latest acquisition was Torre Saracena's most prestigious villa, an enormous three-storey edifice built in the early fifties by Pope Pius XII's personal surgeon. Not that this affluence was evident at his beach establishment. Despite all the improvements – the most recent being a straw-thatched carport for his dark blue Lancia Thema – it remained as always a glorified shack.

Parsimony was an important ingredient of his financial success, as I realised when my *spaghetti alle vongole* arrived and I counted exactly five clams in my sauce. I took my plate straight back to the kitchen, where his wife (who still did most of the cooking) informed me blithely that five was all anybody got nowadays. 'But that's outrageous!' I protested.

'It's not outrageous, it's business,' she said with an artful grin. 'But for old times' sake I'll give you another ladleful.'

My friends' apartment was perfect except for the fact that I could find only two thin army-issue blankets; insufficient for a chilly November night. So the next morning, and still wearing the clothes I had slept in, I took myself off to Saracena Mare in search of something more texturally substantial. I was reluctantly heading for the overpriced Emporio Egidio (Torre Saracena's approximation of a department store) when I spotted a man selling tartan plaids from a battered old Fiat in the forecourt of the Hotel Minerva. They were perfect: cheap, chunky and so cracklingly synthetic they sparked. After some debate I selected one in electric tones of green, yellow and blue.

'Nice colours,' commented a voice behind me and I turned to walk straight into Lena la Ladra's open arms.

Of all the people in the world Lena was one of my least favourite. I would never forgive her for having tried to feed us to the Neapolitan Mafia. Despite this, I found I couldn't hate her, either. It was partly her brazenness, partly her energy, partly the fact we had known each other for so long. Whatever the reason, I felt a definite surge of pleasure at seeing her again.

'If you'd told me you were coming I'd have fixed you up in this new residence I'm managing – free of charge, of course,' she said with a crafty wink. And slipping her arm through mine she swept me back to her office for '*un bel l'aperitivo*' and a chat.

Lena was an inspired gossip. For the next hour or so she regaled me with stories of births, deaths, courtships and marriages as well as separations and adulterous betrayals unthinkable only a decade before. She also told me that her youngest son – the apple of her eye and the child for whom she was most ambitious – had insisted on leaving school to become an apprentice car mechanic.

'We argue all the time,' she complained. '"Stop interfering," he says, "I'm happy as I am." "*Figlio mio*," I tell him, "we were all happy at seventeen – just wait until you're forty!"'

Her biggest gripe, however, was the increasing number of rival estate agents she had to contend with. 'As for buying and selling, the market's static,' she said. 'Over two-thirds of the houses in the old town are either owned by outsiders already or kept by Saracenesi as holiday lets. Nothing moves.'

Benedetta agreed, although the focus of her concern was different. 'There are only two local families living in Via S. Leone now and when the season ends the village empties and we hardly sell a thing. But worse than that is the loneliness. There are some days when mother and I don't see a single soul.'

Her mother was sitting in her usual chair by the door. Despite bad rheumatism she still came in for a part of each day to salt anchovies and stuff olives. 'People say we should move to Saracena Mare like everyone else,' she grunted. 'But life's not better there than it is here.'

'Mother's right,' Benedetta agreed. 'Teenagers hang out in discotheques instead of spending time with their families. Nobody sits on doorsteps or balconies anymore.

The last village *festa* was seven years ago and our sense of community has been destroyed. The village has lost its heart. It's an empty shell.'

'Worse,' said the mother. 'It's a corpse. Its lifeblood has been drained away.'

The full impact of this truth hit me that evening as I walked through the honeycombed alleyways of the deserted town. The silence was sepulchral. No noise of clashing pots or loud radios. No strident voices, no children's laughter, no babies crying. However hard my heart and ears strained, the only sound was the ring of my footsteps on ancient polished stone. And as darkness grew and the houses became long shuttered shadows pressing in on either side, I found myself suspended between dream and reality. I felt like a phantom projection wandering through an empty stage set. Or at least it was empty until my memories came spilling out to fill the spaces. And then Torre Saracena came alive again with all that had once been and would be no more.

www.summersdale.com